IS THE DAY OF THE DENOMINATION DEAD?

IS THE DAY
OF THE
DENOMINATION
DEAD?

BY
ELMER L. TOWNS

THOMAS NELSON INC.
Publishers Since 1798
NASHVILLE • NEW YORK

Published by Thomas Nelson Inc., Nashville, Tennessee,
and simultaneously in Don Mills, Ontario, by
Thomas Nelson & Sons (Canada) Limited.

© 1973 Elmer Towns

Printed in the United States of America

Library of Congress Cataloging in Publication Data
Towns, Elmer L.

Is the Day of the Denomination Dead?

Bibliography: p.

1. Sects—United States.   2. United States—
Religion.   3. Independent Churches—United States.
I. Title.
BR516.5.T68   280′.07′73   73–6993
     ISBN 0–8407–5052–8

DEDICATED TO MY MOTHER

Who put me in Sunday School at age six and saw to it
   that I didn't miss once during the next 14 years
Who had prayer before each meal and heard my prayers
   each night
Who taught me the Bible and the Westminster Shorter
   Catechism
Who insisted that I live by the light I had from the
   Scripture
Who did all that any boy could ever ask of his mother.

Table of Contents

Introduction

The mammoth struggle among churchmen today concerns the very purpose and meaning of the church. A Sunday morning visit to an average American community will reveal various kinds of church services, each of them claiming to reflect the biblical pattern of worship. Many churches are organized around a *worship catalyst,* meaning that here you will receive a printed program, be given a prayer book, be entertained with deep organ tones of classical anthems, hear appropriate prayers read at proper intervals, ending with a short sermon "devotional" on the topic of God.

The next church is likely to be like an *evangelistic tent,* although the sawdust on the floors and rough-hewn benches are missing. The evangelistic singing is bouncy, the announcements are delivered as though by a midway barker, and the sermon is geared at getting people to "walk the aisle for Jesus."

A third type of church one might encounter gives a *classroom lecture.* The person attending might picture himself sitting in an armchair as he listens to the sermon, although chalkboards, globes, and books are absent. The minister sees himself as teacher, sometimes interjecting Greek words or other pedagogical techniques into his Sunday morning sermon.

The next church might be likened unto a *spiritual chamber of commerce.* The pastor, reflecting the sociological elite, might assume that religion is the "in" thing, as "in" people take winter vacations to Florida, or purchase a car for their teenage son.

The next church service resembles a group dynamics *therapy session,* with the minister as the super-psychiatrist. *Koinonia* becomes the catalyst, and honesty is the required initiatory rite. Sometimes called the underground church, such congregations

9

meet in homes, church basements, or hotel dining rooms. The next church resembles the *NAACP pep rally,* and the minister—even though his skin is white—chides his audience for black discrimination. His chief appeal is to the white-black guilt complex, and his major purpose is to kill any vestigial remains of Jim Crow.

The next church is likened unto a *communistic cell gathering.* The minister takes the role of the block leader who spews hatred for imperialism, capitalism, and freedom as the "American-pigs" see it. The sermon is aimed at overthrowing American institutions; some points are subtly made, others mount a frontal attack. Finally, some churches are like *rural school board meetings,* fighting to compete in a modern world. Consolidation is inevitable, but the minister—like the chairman of the school board—tries in every way possible to keep past forms, completely oblivious to the changing world.

A few years ago this struggle over the nature of the church was not evident; most American churches had the same form of worship, although based on different theological distinctives. But with diversity has come dispute: the nature of the church is the topic of theological argument in the 70's. What is the church? What is its purpose? How can the church fulfill the New Testament requirements? Further, as churchmen are criticizing the church, a more venerable target for attack is the denomination.

Have denominations served their function and, like the running board of a car, are no longer needed? Did God ever intend that the church establish denominations? What have they accomplished? How have they hurt the cause of Christ? If denominations are deteriorating . . . why? Who are the dying denominations? These questions demand answers.

God Blesses the Local Church

This book was not written as an exposé of Protestant religious bodies, but the author is convinced that God's primary blessing is upon the local church. He sees a number of vibrant churches carrying out the Great Commission, these churches are not associated with denominations. They are independent, yet they are growing. He notes that the old mainline denominations are not expanding. Some evangelical denominations are struggling. The ugly question keeps poking its head into his thinking: "Is there something inhibitive about denominations?"

If denominations were not ordained of God, what place do they have in spreading the gospel?

The author is not against denominations. He agrees with the contributions of denominations to the cause of Christ noted by Noel Smith (see chapter 4 and 5). However, the author is against denominationalism (the abuses of denominations) and raises a demanding question: Was denominational cooperation ever in the plan of God (see chapter 4)?

This manuscript is not concerned with the deterioration among the Roman Catholics, but rather with the mainline Protestant church groups of America who go by the accepted title *denomination*. The differences between Roman Catholicism and Protestantism is overwhelming in nature, even though there are similarities in form. Both Protestant denominations and Roman Catholicism are declining in attendance. Some of the same reasons for deterioration are evident in both groups. However, an accurate study of the decline of Roman Catholicism would have to deal with the nature of the Catholic Church, which will not be attempted here. Beyond all of the sociological reasons for the demise of the Catholic Church, the author feels God has never blessed the movement. Roman Catholicism has never met the requirements of the New Testament, whereas many Protestant denominations in the non-Catholic world met the New Testament requirement and purpose at one time.

Is Liberalism at Fault?

The author is not condemning all denominations, nor is he saying that all denominations are dying; this is simply not the case. To be accurate, we must realize that statistics are somewhat variable. Most of the mainline denominations are declining, especially those mainline denominations that have a bent towards liberal theology. However, not every church in a denomination considered liberal, is, in fact, liberal. Some are quite fundamental in doctrine. On the other side of the coin, most fundamental denominations are growing in strength and size, yet the variable statistics tell us that some fundamental denominations are not growing. To be accurate, some individual churches within the fundamental or evangelical denominations have liberal tendencies. Therefore, what is the answer? We will attempt to step back and view the entire religious scene, showing that mainline denominations are generally declining whereas fundamentalist denominations are generally growing.

This book deals only with American churches, for several reasons. First, there is no other nation in history quite like the United States. We are a nation created by liberty, individualism, and revolt against European forms. Our nation is nurtured by pragmatism, industrialism, mass media, and mobility; creating conditions in which the church/denomination thrives or dies. Every church is a product of its times and culture. The American church is no different. Therefore, most of the conclusions in this book can be applied only to the churches in America. Even though some conditions might apply abroad, the reader must be careful not to judge foreign churches by the unique culture of churches in the United States.

The second reason this book is oriented to America is that no other country has statistics available like those found in the United States. Our computers spitting out statistics have helped us see trends in the making. Thus, the book takes liberty in making certain observations that could not be made earlier. Statistics were not available when the decline among the Protestant churches in England took place. It is almost as though the church world woke up and found their pews empty, then asked the question, "Why?" It was then too late to reverse the trend; the vacant sanctuary was a matter of fact.

Is the Denominational Day Dying?

Is the day of denomination past? The indicator shows a new breeze blowing through Christian churches. The movement is not yet a rushing mighty wind. Denominations seem to be sailing upwind; they are pointed in the wrong direction, and their future will be more difficult. They that live by the sword shall die by the sword. Denominations that were born in doctrinal battles shall see their life snatched away by the theological sword.

I would like to give recognition to those who have made a contribution to this book. (Authors are supposed to do so.) But I don't want to blame anyone for the brash accusations I have made, nor would anyone want credit for the obvious conclusions that have been presented. I have simply written the things I have seen and heard in the church.

Appreciation is expressed to Alden Laird for doing the research on chapter 2; to Mrs. Marie Chapman for editing and proofreading the copy; and to Beverly Grooms for typing the manuscript.

I doubt if any denomination will vote itself out of existence and liquidate the assets as a result of reading this book. I even doubt if any denominational official will resign. My prayer is that some churches will ponder their rush into denominational deterioration. I will be happy if pastors and laymen will realize that every step toward centralization of power is another trigger pull in the game of religious Russian roulette.

This is the day of the local church and if this book helps to strengthen individual New Testament congregations, it will accomplish its purpose.

Sincerely yours in Christ,
ELMER L. TOWNS

CHAPTER 1

Churches Without a Denomination

Akron Baptist Temple

The late Dr. Dallas Billington built the largest Sunday School in the world with no outside help. The Akron (Ohio) Baptist Temple grew out of the heart of Billington when he put in a ten-hour workday in a rubber factory during Depression days, having come out of hills of Kentucky. Young Billington led a number of men to Jesus Christ, and each day at lunch he would pull a small dog-eared New Testament out of his overalls and teach his converts. He instructed them to attend a Baptist church.

"We don't understand these Yankee preachers," replied one of his followers.

"Why don't you start a church? I like to hear you explain the Bible," another spoke up.

Billington was tall, muscular, and considered good-looking; he turned to the foreman, J. Stanley Bond: "I'll preach and you run the Sunday School; stick with me and we'll build the largest church in the world."

They did!

The church began in Reimer School on Manchester Road, Easter Sunday, 1934. The first collection totalled $1.18. Thirteen people were present. Stanley Bond opened Sunday School that first day and continues as its leader until this time. Average attendance reached 6,300 in 1969.

Dallas Billington went to be with the Lord August 26, 1972. He died as he lived, riding high in the saddle; his Sunday School was the largest in America. A month later, the First Baptist Church, Hammond, Indiana, overtook the Ohio Sunday School and was recognized by *Christian Life* magazine as the largest in our nation.

Billington scorned denominational help and fellowship during his 38 years of ministry. He believed it was not necessary. Billington could never have followed a denominational minister's manual; he was too independent. When young ministers came to him for guidance he replied, "Use this"—patting his Bible.

"Believe it! You can't sell something you are not sold on yourself."

Billington was the epitome of rugged individualism. He told young men to fill their minds with the Bible, fill their hearts with faith, then go to a town, knock on doors, and build a church.

"Nell and I could do it again," he told a reporter. "All I would need is a store building, chairs, hymnbooks, and strength to knock on doors and lead people to Christ."

Today the Akron Baptist Temple occupies an enormous six-wing $9 million complex at 2324 Manchester Road, with an annual budget of over $1 million, a testimony that churches can be built without denominational backing or affiliation.

Thomas Road Baptist Church

Thirty-five people began the Thomas Road Baptist Church, Lynchburg, Va., on June 25, 1956, and God has done there more unthinkable miracles than the thirty-five in their wildest imagination ever expected. Sixteen years later, Sunday School attendance averaged over 7,000, with the largest reported Sunday School since Pentecost, when 19,020 people assembled on June 26, 1972.

That first handful of people were dedicated to constructing buildings, taking offerings, baptizing people, and all the other necessary requirements to forge out a New Testament Church. They began in a bankrupt concrete-block bottling plant, cut the weeds, washed cola syrup off the walls, and sat on old theater seats. The room held only 100 comfortably.

The people shared the vision of Jerry Falwell, their first and only pastor, to reach lost people for Jesus Christ. Twenty-three-year-old Falwell, a home town boy, was right out of Baptist Bible College, Springfield, Missouri. He began knocking on every door in the neighborhood. As Falwell grew in maturity, the Sunday

School expanded in size, and the congregation enlarged in vision.

A radio program was aired, and it expanded to other stations. Within six months "The Old-Time Gospel Hour" was televised on Saturday afternoons. Next, a ministry to alcoholic men was established on a farm in Appomattox, Virginia. Afterwards, new ventures exploded into existence. Treasure Island Youth Camp was offered free to any and all children; Hope Aglow Mission was begun for men behind bars; Lynchburg Christian Academy, with grades K through 12, Lynchburg Baptist College, Thomas Road Bible Institute, and Lynchburg Baptist Theological Seminary completed the educational offerings. A family counseling ministry was opened.

Falwell taught the congregation to tithe from the first Sunday, according to Percy Hall, the only chairman the deacons have ever had. This past year income from all sources reached over $10 million. This one local church has a budget larger than many denominations.

Today the Sunday morning service is telecast over 450 TV stations in the U.S., Canada, Japan, and other foreign countries; the daily radio program is heard over 100 stations; 3,000 children attend camp free; Elim Home for Alcoholics has free dormitory space for 18 men; over 700 children attend the Academy, and 1400 students are registered in the college and Bible Institute.

The Thomas Road Baptist Church has a worldwide all-embracing outreach. The local church has replaced the function of a denomination, and Falwell teaches that all young preachers should build a super-aggressive church.

Falwell explains, "If I followed the direction of a denomination, we would be running 300 in attendance today."

First Baptist Church, Dallas, Texas

Dr. W. A. Criswell, First Baptist Church, Dallas, Texas, pastors the largest church in the Southern Baptist Convention, which is the largest Protestant denomination in America. The church now averages over 5,500 in Sunday School; it was averaging 800 when Criswell came. As former president of the Southern Baptist Convention, Criswell voiced for his church, "We are an independent Baptist church in fellowship with the Southern Baptist

Convention." Putting his independent tendency into action, Criswell has stopped using some of the Southern Baptist Sunday School literature, has limited giving to the Cooperative Program, and has been vocally critical of liberal trends in Nashville, Tennessee. Criswell told this author, "Our church doesn't need the Southern Baptist Convention, they need us." He went on to explain that the Southern Baptist Convention needed a strong conservative church to be an example to the other churches in the Convention. He wants to build a powerful church that will teach the Word of God and stand against liberalism. He indicated a true New Testament church would govern its own affairs, rather than being led around through the nose by denominational bureaucrats. He continued, "I am not a watchdog nor a conscience to the Southern Baptist Convention. I am trying to build the First Baptist Church into what every Southern Baptist church should become." According to one observer, "Criswell will probably stay in the Convention, even though he sees its faults."

First Baptist, Hammond, Indiana

Dr. Jack Hyles, pastor, First Baptist Church, Hammond, Indiana, speaks with bitterness in his voice regarding the Southern Baptist Convention. Years ago, he was dropped from the rolls by the local Association of the Southern Baptist Convention when he was trying to build a church in Texas. Hyles took some classes at Southwestern Baptist Theological Seminary, Fort Worth, Texas, a Southern Baptist-sponsored school. Hyles realizes that the Convention can muscle around a young preacher-boy as he was, but will say nothing against a giant like Criswell. Hyles sees a vicious trend toward liberalism in the Southern Baptist Convention, compounded by the political bourgeoisie. He is happy *not* to be part of any denomination. Jack Hyles first built the Miller Road Baptist Church, Garland, Texas, from approximately 100 to an average of 1,200 in Sunday School. In 1959 he accepted the pastorate of First Baptist Church, Hammond, Indiana, which was averaging 800 in attendance. The church was a member of the American Baptist Convention, but the congregation voted to disassociate denominational ties.

The church grew under Hyles's aggressive leadership, reaching an average attendance of over 10,000 in the Spring of 1973.

Sunday School meets at 9:45 and 11:00 a.m. and over 100 Sunday School buses weekly bring 4,000 riders to study the Word of God. The church has 250 students enrolled in a class for retarded pupils, 100 for the hard-of-hearing, and 80 in a Spanish-speaking class.

The runaway success of the Hammond church stands to indict denominationalism. Hyles was one of them until they voted him out; now he does not need a denomination and would reject any assistance from them.

Florence, South Carolina

Three years ago, Bill Monroe left a comfortable position in Indianapolis, Indiana, because he felt the call of God to start a church in South Carolina. Monroe was 25 years of age and had read in *The Ten Largest Sunday Schools* that Dallas Billington had built the largest Sunday School in the world, Akron (Ohio) Baptist Temple. Monroe figured that if Billington could build a great church, so could he. Monroe had finished three and a half years of business education at the University of South Carolina, but had never preached a sermon. He felt an inner compulsion to build a church. He loaded his furniture on a Ryder Rental truck, moved to Florence, S.C., and began preaching in a deserted theater on an abandoned military base.

Attendance grew in the abandoned movie house until it reached 200, but facilities were woefully inadequate. The young church had only $1,000 in its building fund, and that was paid down on the purchase of 10 acres of property on four-lane U.S. 301, south of the city. Because Monroe was a soul-winner, a number of individuals found Christ in the going, growing church. They were committed to the future of the church. The church sold a $200,000 bond issue locally to the members and friends of the church. Since Monroe was a business major in college, he understood the requirements for an adequate operation. He used the bond money for the following purchases:

Land	$ 40,000
Building & interest	141,800
Hard-top	5,000
Driveway & Parking	5,000
Illuminated sign	2,200
Printing Press & equipment	2,500
Office equipment	1,500
School desks, chalkboards	2,000
	$200,000

Monroe looked to God to supply his finances, and by faith through prayer he believed God would provide all his needs. His present $2,000 weekly offering is more than adequate to pay off indebtedness, operate the church with four full-time employees, and finance expanding ministries. Monroe indicates that God met his needs because he obeyed the biblical principles of building a church. He feels that a denomination is both unnecessary and unbiblical.

Three years later, Sunday School averaged 500, weekly offering averaged $2,000, the congregation had built an auditorium seating 500 and is now constructing an 1100-seat auditorium that will be finished by their fourth anniversary. Monroe built the Florence Baptist Temple in the shadow of several Southern Baptist churches and is now larger than most of them. He began his church because he felt that the others were dead and had no soul-winning outreach into the community. According to Monroe's testimony, denominational backing would have hindered the growth of his church. "I didn't need their financing or encouragement." He went on to observe, "If I had had to follow the direction of a district superintendent, I would never have begun."

Garland, Texas

The Lavon Drive Baptist Church, Garland, Texas, needed financing to construct a 2,200-seat auditorium, classrooms to expand its Sunday School, and facilities to expand its Christian day school. The church also needed additional capital to refinance its present mortgage and purchase ground for expansion. Usually, a denominational church contacts headquarters, which helps arrange for a loan. This church is independent of all religious affiliation; twelve years ago a group of men met in Blaylock's Nursery to pray about starting a church. The following week the new congregation met in a deserted store where pleasure boats had been sold. Without outside help, the congregation raised money, bought property, built its first building, and began evangelizing the community. The church purchased buses to bring children to Sunday School and built four more buildings in the next ten years. Presently, Sunday School is averaging over 1,200. Thirty-three-year-old Gary Coleman has been leading the church for the past seven years. He took the pastorate when attendance averaged 250. The church has a $228,739 annual budget and recently completed an $800,000 bond sale; many members sold bonds to their friends and neighbors throughout Garland. Pastor Gary Coleman indicates that freedom from denominational help forced the congregation to rely on the Lord; it has made the church stronger than would otherwise be expected. When it comes to financing, Coleman doesn't need Convention backing.

Savannah, Georgia

The Bible Baptist Church, Savannah, Georgia, was begun 17 years ago on the west side of the city near a low-rental housing project, considered the slums of the town. Out of a humble living room has come the largest church in the city and an energetic home missions outreach. Pastor Cecil Hodges is committed to helping start independent Baptist churches, having assisted eleven churches financially. In 1970 Rev. Carl Baugh was put on the home missions budget of the Savannah Church and sent to St. Louis, Missouri, to start an independent Baptist church. The Savannah congregation gave more than money; the people backed the work by prayer.

St. Louis

Carl Baugh pulled his Chevy station wagon into Saint Louis on a late Friday evening in August, 1970, and within two hours found four acres of ground located on I–244 and Page Avenue Expressway. Baugh knew that a church must be at the center of population to reach the Midwest city; 90,000 cars a day passed that location. He took an option on the $90,000 property and secured a lease on North Junior High School, half a block away. Church services were held there until the infant congregation could build on the new property. Baugh knocked on doors, leading people to Jesus Christ. Within three months, a church of 27 people had been gathered and on November 23, 1969, Pastor Cecil Hodges flew to Saint Louis to organize the Calvary Heights Baptist Temple.

Hodges does not give money to a denomination to help start churches; he feels one church should give direct support to another. Hodges indicates that if finances pass through headquarters, his church loses the burden of responsibility and the joy of accomplishment. Hodges believes that if every church would help start another church, there would be no necessity for denominations.

Building a Great Church

Baugh has built a great church, now averaging over 500 in Sunday School, with a yearly budget of $100,000. The church has a 400-seat auditorium and total investments now worth $1,200,000, an amazing capital report for a three-year-old congregation. Baugh believes a denomination's help could not have been as effective as the friendship of another local church. On several occasions, Hodges preached in the young church, and when Baugh had difficulties, he picked up the phone and called Hodges to get immediate suggestions for solving his problems.

Jerry Falwell has often advised young preachers to get a printing press as one of the first pieces of new equipment the church should buy. He notes that the Communists and cults use the printed page to circulate their message, so he reasons, "Why should the church not saturate through the printed page?" In the early days, Falwell had a small offset press and one employee, Ray Treadway, as printer. The church was running less than 500, yet Falwell printed a newspaper and mailed the gospel to every name he could get on the mailing list. In addition, Falwell printed his Sunday School lessons, booklets, tracts, letterheads, and sermons.

Rather than depend on literature from a denominational publishing house, he printed his own material and today claims that every young pastor should follow his example.

"P.O. Box Four Aces"

George Hogan had been arrested so many times he couldn't remember the number of times he had been in jail. As he sat on his bunk in a Virginia chain gang, he picked up a tract off the floor. Jerry Falwell's name was there, but the address had been torn off. Because Falwell had saturated the area through radio, television, and printed page, the other convicts immediately recognized the name Falwell and knew his address in Lynchburg: "P.O. Box Four Aces" (a gambling term to mean 1111). Hogan was saved, his life was changed, and today he is head of the mail operations for Thomas Road Baptist Church and the Old-Time Gospel Hour.

Four years ago the author researched the ten largest Sunday Schools in America and found that seven out of ten churches did not use Sunday School literature from a publishing house, but used the Bible only. The pastors prepared and printed Bible outlines rather than use outside help.

The author moderated a panel for publication in *Christian Life* Magazine, "What kind of Sunday School Material Should You Use?" (June, 1970). Bill Greig, Jr., vice president of Gospel Light Publications, talked with Dr. Warren Weirsby, formerly of Calvary Baptist Church (attendance 1,000), Covington, Kentucky, and Dr. John Rawlings, Landmark Baptist Temple (attendance 5,000), Cincinnati, Ohio. Neither of the pastors used literature but prepared their own. Weirsby stated he wrote his own Sunday School literature because: (1) the minister feeds his flock by providing Bible for all ages; (2) an outside publishing firm couldn't know the needs of his people as does the pastor. Rawlings added a critical reason: (3) Sunday School literature is the instrument used by the liberals to corrupt a church. He pointed to the deterioration within the American Baptist Convention due to watering-down the Bible in Sunday School literature. The gray-haired Rawlings, known as "the war-horse for fundamentalism," vehemently maintains that a denomination is unbiblical.

Falwell adds another reason for printing his own Sunday School lessons: all of the family studies the same lesson at the same time, eventually covering the Bible every four years. There is no denominational literature that teaches the same lesson from kindergarten to adult level. Falwell sees the splintering effect of a different lesson for each age. Also, he points out that printed literature usually leaves out great gaps of the Bible. He advertises, "the Bible is our only curriculum."

Christian colleges and seminaries traditionally have been founded by denominations because local churches have not been financially strong enough to attempt the unthinkable task. But today super-aggressive churches are starting colleges and seminaries at the rate of one a week. Recently the author made a list of 61 colleges founded in the last two years in independent churches.

Baptist World University began last year in New Testament Baptist Church (attendance 2,500), Miami, Florida, and several years ago Heritage College was founded in Scott Memorial Baptist Church (attendance 1,000), San Diego, California.

Some colleges are small and anemic, with a small student body, such as Springfield Baptist College located in the Baptist Temple, Springfield, Mo., with 14 students; the church staff and surrounding pastors comprise the faculty. Even though small, we must admire their individualistic vision and tenacious determinism.

A Major Christian College

One of the largest is Lynchburg Baptist College, begun in 1971 with a total matriculation of 305 in the first year, swelling to over 1,400 full- and part-time students the following year.

The college was founded by Jerry Falwell, pastor of Thomas Road Baptist Church, in the church facilities, with assistance of many church staff members, but reaching the next year 29 full-time faculty members, 16 part-time, and a budget of $1,250,000.

The Lynchburg college has seven major fields of study and operates on a concept of shared services with the church. The $2 million TV equipment owned by the church is used in the Communications major; the music equipment of the church is shared with the college, and students taking an education major practice teach in Lynchburg Christian Academy. The church's computer is used by the college registrar's office.

All students were given a free trip to Israel during the first year, as part of the "action-oriented" curriculum, to study Bible geography on site. The second year, students were given a trip to England to study the Wesley revival and the beginning of the Sunday School.

Falwell confesses the free trip has not attracted the large number of students to his unaccredited school, it is the biblical distinctives. "Our boys look like boys, and our girls wear their dresses like young ladies," he announces over TV. The college has high moral standards for the students.

"We have a large group of students from Southern Baptist churches, because their schools have lost their doctrinal distinctives, and their students dress like bums," replies the pastor. Falwell knows the college will continue to grow because many denominational churches have no conservative alternate for college education.

This year the Thomas Road Baptist Church is beginning a theological seminary and expects over 100 young men holding an approved baccalaureate college degree to enter for preparation for the ministry. When most mainline denominational seminaries have declining attendance, Lynchburg Baptist Theological Seminary is getting off the ground. Many other evangelical seminaries are growing.

Churches Grow, Denominations Decline

America is witnessing the explosive growth of a vast number of churches, each of them super-aggressive in its outreach. These growing churches are making mockery of the downward indicator of denominational churches. *Christian Life* magazine estimates there are 10,000 such churches in America. In a day when mainline denominational churches are losing numbers, seeing attendance dwindle, and feeling a financial pinch, such churches, a new breed, are proving that they don't need denominations.

The Protestant denominations of America provide money to help build new churches and give counsel to help pastors start new congregations. These super-aggressive churches don't need denominational help.

Denominations have written ministerial handbooks, "the discipline" to guide young preachers through complex social and theological problems. Also, education and inspiration is provided by the annual meeting of the denomination. These self-motivating churches don't need denominational direction and inspiration.

Another service of denominations is literature and Sunday School quarterlies to reinforce their doctrinal distinctives. Also, the denominations provide other services, as: pension funds for retired ministers, denominational colleges and seminaries, home and foreign mission boards, committees for social action, and a number of lesser ministries. These independent churches don't want denominational services.

Who are these super-aggressive churches and where are they found? Statistics show that liberal-oriented denominations are declining, while conservatives are growing. Six years ago I began listing the 100 largest Sunday Schools in *Christian Life* magazine. Nine of the ten largest were independent of denominational ties. The independent churches are evidently the largest and fastest growing in America.

Conclusion

The massive growth of super-aggressive churches does not make a case against denominations. Their strength only illustrates that "there is a better way." The very fact these pastors are working successfully outside denominations is a backhanded slap at denominationalism. They don't want in—they want out. Some of these pastors are neutral or apathetic; they ignore denominational structure. Other pastors are militant against denominations. One minister, when interviewed for this book, echoed his prejudice: "It's about time the fat cats in headquarters get it."

- **The Thomas Road Baptist Church doesn't need a denomination.**
- **Dr. W. A. Criswell doesn't need the Southern Baptist Convention.**
- **10,000 super-aggressive churches don't accept bureaucracy.**
- **Does America need denominations?**

NOTES

1. The author coined the phrase *super-aggressive evangelism* after seeing the example of Jerry Falwell and hearing his definition of saturation evangelism "preaching the gospel by every available means, to every available person, at every available time."

CHAPTER 2

The Church Hangover

The Protestant church "bust" of the 50's brought a warm glow to the hearts of churchmen. The future was rosy, and all indicators pointed upward. Church membership reached an all-time high, and offerings were greater than ever. Some perhaps even believed that America could be a Christian nation in reality.

A decade later, gloom settled over denominational offices. The rosy prospects of the Kingdom had wilted. Worried church officials watched the arrows edge downward in "nickels and noses," the twin indicative thermostats to measure religious fervency. Attendance was off, and offerings were down.

Disillusionment spread through the members of the Episcopal Cathedral of Saint John the Divine of New York. Work on the magnificent new ediface, begun with hope and congregational pride, was halted. As membership went down, the church faced the question: Why build a larger and more expensive building? The Right Reverend Horace W. B. Donegan announced that the unfinished structure would stand as a symbol of the agony of the city until human needs were met.

Did the church leaders take a cop-out? What did the jagged walls symbolize? Was concern for the needs of the city only a rationalization, or was the new theology of social action beginning to add scalps to its belt?

Newsmen baptized the sixties "a violent decade." Americans witnessed perhaps more change than in any other ten-year period of history. The mass student riots of Berkeley, along with the shootings at the University of Mississippi and Kent State, told us something was wrong with our society. Violence shocked the nation through the slaughter of John F. Kennedy, his brother

Bobby, followed by Martin Luther King and the growing crime rate, including forcible rape and robbery. Burning draft cards flashed lawlessness to the nation's living rooms. The Boston Strangler silently perpetuated the sickness. Where was the church when our nation needed her most?

Education was embroiled in turmoil; school desegregation riots in Detroit raised questions about public schools; coeducational housing on college campuses repudiated the Protestant ethic; and "God is dead" theology continued the doubts in theological seminaries. For the first time in history, teachers walked out on strike.

The sixties saw an avalanche of anti-establishment and counter-culture literature. With new freedom, raw pornography was sold in "Adult only" book stores, and *Playboy*, a runaway sexcuss, increased from 1,000,000 circulation in 1960 to 5,000,000 in 1970. Playboy clubs flourished. The church seemed powerless to stay an apparent moral erosion.

Where Was the Church?

Bob Dylan and Joan Baez were idolized for their protest songs, and the rock festivals flagrantly paraded nudity and narcotics. *Jesus Christ Superstar* rocketed to a multimillion-dollar enterprise. We invented the rating for movies, then, with an "X marks the spot," allowed women to undress, couples to copulate, and, finally, deviates to pollute the imaginations of man. Homosexuality and lesbianism became popular themes on the screen. What was not thought acceptable became "seeable" in "I Am Curious Yellow." Why didn't the church attempt to counter the tide?

Life in the supermarket and high schools changed. Miniskirts were in, LSD was taken, Timothy Leary became a college hero, the hippie drop-out was encouraged. Johnny Carson was allowed to swear on TV. Profanity increased. Where was the church?

The Berlin Wall separated nations; the Cuban Crisis separated hemispheres. Vietnam was a hot war, and the Middle East was a stand-off. China emerged as a world power. Nuclear weapons were stockpiled by nations ready to tinder the powder keg. When the nations needed her, where was the church?

The U.S. Supreme Court outlawed required prayer and Bible reading. Clergymen abandoned the ministry. Secularism as typified by Harvey Cox's *The Secular City* ran rampant through churches. Why did the church love those who were raping her?

America needed the church greater during the sixties than ever before. When awakened for the battle, the church appeared as a drunken fighter, ploying at shadowy images. The church had a hangover.

The indicator pointed down. None was more grave than the Gallup Opinion Index, covering a 13-year period, asking the following question to a cross-section of adults across America: "At the present time, do you think religion as a whole is increasing its influence on American life, or losing its influence?" The graph reveals popular opinion, which represents all religions in proportion to their number of followers.

%

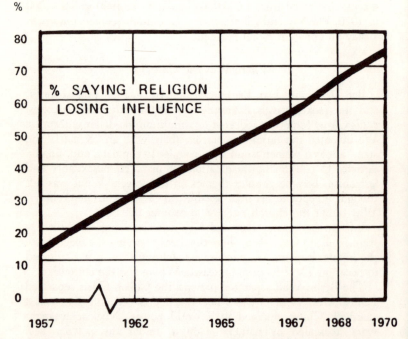

A board of directors carefully studies graphs and charts to determine future policy. The opinion charts have been going down for 15 years, the attendance graphs for five years. Church

officials seem to be unconcerned and unwilling to change policies to reverse the trend. Perhaps the above analogy is wrong. Maybe the denominational officials are not the board of directors; the actual board is the people, and they have voted by absentee ballot.

Since 1957, seven surveys on this subject have dramatically revealed a sharp and steady decline in the public's confidence in religion. In 1957, only 14 percent held the opinion that religion was losing its influence, as compared to a staggering 75 percent in 1970. The 1970 survey revealed that three out of every four adults believe that religion as a whole was losing its influence on American life.[2]

Then again, God may be the ultimate board member. Church officials will have to wait until eternity to find out how He voted in the sixties. The author is of the opinion they could have known through His revelation, the Scriptures.

According to the Gallup audit: "The latest survey findings represent one of the most dramatic reversals in opinion in the history of polling."[3] Three decades ago few criticized the church; it was held in esteem, along with motherhood, Congress, and Saturday night in town. But those days are gone. The church is now fair game for any with a self-made soap box. Gallup revealed that Americans believe religion is losing its influence for these reasons: (1) The church is "outdated," (2) "It is not relevant in today's world," (3) "Morals are breaking down," and (4) "People are becoming more materialistic."[4] Whether these are surface problems or root causes will be examined later. The import of these statistics is that the people *believe* them, and people make up a church.

Is the Church Relevant?

Although some of the public's reasons appear to be contradictory, a growing pessimism about the church is apparent as was true of this typical response by a 36-year-old Dallas housewife: "The Church is totally out of step with the times. It is a medieval institution trying to hang on in the twentieth century. It's a hopeless struggle."[5] In response to the question, "Is organized religion a relevant part of your life at the present time or not?"

Fifty-eight percent of the college students interviewed responded that it is not.[6]

In all probability, the average American would say he is "religious," or that he is "Christian"; however, this is not a vote of confidence in organized religion. Most Americans do not believe the church is meeting the needs of our present-day society. John A. Olthuis comments, "Very few among the 45,000,000 name-Christians in North America really believe that Christianity can change the world; that Christianity alone can straighten out the world-wide mess."[7]

To be fair, many church papers screamed "Wolf!" But the religious readers were not aroused. The modern-day Jeremiahs were alarmed about the church and about our country's future. They seemed too ineffective and irrelevent to make an impact on events that make history. During this period of greatest danger, the church melted into a comfortable compromise with the world. Many Americans slipped into indifference concerning religious life, believing that the supernatural God could not effect natural events.

They believed God had no adequate voice to solve the problems of a "messed-up world." Thus, the shift of attention to a social-oriented ministry, away from the mystery of the Godhead. Frustrated by the seemingly unsolvable world problems, a negative reaction toward organized religion occurred.

Sterilization of Religion

Compromise, indifference, and secularism have all plagued sterilized religion during the sixties. The institutional church failed to exercise a leading role in the community, and as a result has become preoccupied with maintaining an equilibrium within itself. Many denominations are in a life-and-death struggle of self-strangulation. The church appears to fight the wrong battle by fighting itself. Olthuis says,

> I believe that the institutional church in America has failed because—with no denominational and few local exceptions—it is so concerned with the coming of the kingdom of the institutional church, that it has lost sight of the vision

of the Kingdom of Jesus Christ—a Kingdom whose coming the church must prophetically proclaim.

Christians who are unconcerned about the state of the institutional church have lost sight of the importance of that church. The more important one considers the institutional church, the more one demands from it, and the more one feels constrained to express alarm when *the church* is suffering.[8]

The latest figures indicate that only 40 percent of the adults of all American faiths attended church on an average week. This has been the result of a steady downward decline since the apex attained in 1955, when 49 percent of adults attended church in a typical week. (Gallup is considered the most accurate of all polls on church attendance.) The question asked of 3,997 people in 300 selected sampling points was: "Did you, yourself, happen to attend church in the last seven days?" Below are the results in churchgoing in the U.S. since the Gallup Poll began making regular audits in 1955. Thirty-six percent of all Protestants attended church in a typical week, compared to 57 percent for the Catholic faith. The national average was 40 percent.

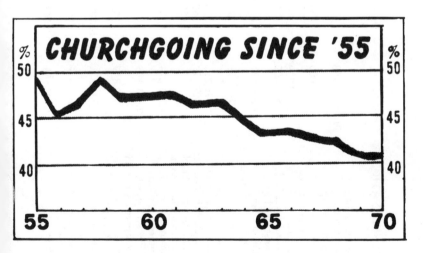

DENOMINATION	1960	1966	1968	1969	1970		
1. American Bapt. Convention	('59) 1,543,198	1,538,988 ('67)	1,454,965		1,472,478	− 66,510	4.3%
2. American Bapt. Assoc.	648,000	731,000	745,620	782,902	786,536	+ 55,536	7.6%
3. American Lutheran Church	2,242,259	2,566,581	2,576,105	2,559,588	2,543,293	− 23,288	0.9%
4. Assemblies of God	508,602	576,058		626,660 ('71)	625,027	+ 48,959	8.5%
5. Christian Church (Dis. of Christ)	1,801,821	1,894,927	1,592,609	1,444,465	1,424,479	− 470,479	24.8%
6. Christian Reformed Church	242,593	275,530	281,523	284,737	285,628	+ 10,098	3.7%
7. Church of God (Cleveland, Tenn.)	170,261	220,405	243,532	257,995	272,276	+ 51,871	23.5%
8. Church of the Nazarene	307,629	350,882	364,789	372,943	383,284	+ 32,402	9.2%
9. The Episcopal Church		3,429,153	3,373,890	3,330,272	3,285,826	− 143,327	4.2%
10. Lutheran Churches in America	2,385,224	3,147,959	3,279,517	*3,135,684	3,106,844	− 41,115	1.3%
11. Lutheran Church (Missouri Synod)	2,391,195	2,729,897	2,781,892	2,786,102	2,788,536	+ 58,639	2.1%
12. Presbyterian Church in U.S.A.	902,849	955,402	961,767	957,569	958,195	− 3,572	0.4%
13. Southern Bapt. Convention	9,731,591	10,947,389	11,330,481	11,487,708	11,628,032	+ 680,643	6.2%
14. Unitarian–Universalists Assoc.	101,205 ('65)	166,622	283,000	265,408		− 17,592	6.2%
15. United Church of Christ	1,427,863	2,063,481	2,032,648	1,997,898	1,960,608	− 102,873	4.9%

DENOMINATION	1960	1966	1968	1969	1970		
16. The United Methodist Church	9,893,094	10,310,619	10,590,720	10,824,010	10,671,774	− 318,946	2.9%
17. The United Pentecostal Church, Inc.	175,000 ('65)	125,000	225,000	200,000		− 25,000	11.1%
18. The United Presby. Church in U.S.	3,259,011	3,298,583	3,222,663	3,165,490	3,087,213	− 211,370	6.4%
19. Wisconsin Evang. Lutheran Synod	235,073 ('64)	358,466		376,319	381,321	+ 22,855	6.4%
20. Church of the Brethren	199,947	191,402	187,957	185,198	182,614	− 8,788	4.5%
21. Nat'l. Assoc. of Cong. Christian Ch.		110,000	110,000		85,000	− 25,000	22.7%
22. Conservative Bapt. Ass. of America	300,000 ('65)	325,000	300,000		300,000	− 25,000	7.7%
23. African Meth. Epis. Zion Church	770,000 ('65) ('59)	1,100,000	879,421		940,000	− 160,000	14.5%
24. Christian & Missionary Alliance	59,657	68,829	119,826	120,330	112,519	− 7,307	6.1%

* Lutheran Church in America is lower because in 1969 Canadian statistics were removed.

Although the Protestant decline in attendance has remained fairly constant, the Catholics have declined 17 points from a high of 74 percent attendance in 1955, as compared to the 1972 figure of 57 percent in church each week.

This corresponds with a survey taken of Detroit area residents which clearly revealed that a sharp and steady decline in church attendance has occurred during the last 15 years. The number of those interviewed who never attend, rose from 10 to 17 percent. In addition, those who believe they have the right to question what the church teaches rose from 68 to 81 percent.[10]

An 18-year-old sophomore at Western Michigan University reported, "I believe in God, but I haven't found a church I am satisfied with. I can't see how churchgoing relates to living a good life."

The drop in attendance explains the apparent static state of church membership in the majority of the largest U.S. denominations. Church membership in most Protestant denominations reached its peak during the ten-year period between 1955 and 1965. In a study of 24 of the largest Protestant denominations during the five-year span between 1965 and 1970, 16 of the 24 bodies declined in membership. Only eight recorded an increase, most of which were slight compared to earlier growth periods.

The alarming fact is that this downward trend appears to be gaining momentum. Interestingly, denominational mergers have increased but have not seemed to curtail this decline.

In a 1972 typical United Methodist Conference in Virginia, the Reverend Ralph E. Haugh, conference statistician, recorded a total of 11,344 "removed by Change Conference Action or Withdrawn." That was 2,290 more than a year ago. While membership dipped sharply, so attendance also declined. This is the trend since 1969.

> We are getting used to this trend, but the trend seems to be becoming a movement. When we began in 1972, we had only 1,100 more members than the former Methodist Conference alone had in 1968. During the past 12 months, we managed to drop significantly below that figure. This week's report indicates people are not leaving the Virginia Conference in droves. They just are not coming in.

Church school membership dipped down 7,486 in the United Methodist Conference from 1971, and church school attendance averaged 103,805, a drop of 4,499 from a year ago. Also included were the fact that the decrease was spread across all age groups.[12]

Children's enrollments,	
as others, down	3,861
Youth, down	1,267
Adults, down	2,187
Leaders, down	171

Theologically conservative denominations generally reveal modest gains, while the more liberal institutions show declines. Among those who increased are: The Church of God (Cleveland, Tennessee), The General Association of Regular Baptists, The Church of the Nazarene, The Assembly of God, and the American Baptist Association.

Among those bodies who declined are: The Christian Church (Disciples of Christ), The United Methodist Church, Lutheran Churches in America, The United Church of Christ, the United Presbyterian Church in the U.S.A., and The Unitarian-Universalists Association. Eleven of the 24 bodies have decreased since 1966 and five have gone down since 1968.

Individual denominational statistics markedly reveal this decline. The American Baptist Convention, according to *Yearbook of American Churches,* in 1959 reported 6,262 churches as compared to only 6,090 in 1970, a decline of nearly 3 percent.

In the 1971 annual tally, the membership of 230 church bodies rose to an all-time high of 128,505,084. However, this is only a .03 percent gain over the previous year's gain of 1.6 percent. The significance here is that this is far below the general population increase of 11 percent. The 1969 data reflects the figures that 62.4 percent of Americans held church membership, but this is below the 63.1 percent in 1968.[13]

Zero for Religion?

The National Council of Churches published a report in 1971 showing that, for the first time since World War II, organized religion in the U.S. has finally reached the point of zero population growth. As an example, the Roman Catholics in 1970 suffered their first membership loss (1,149) since 1900. The loss of population is marginal, but the fact they are going down is significant. In 1970, too, the National Conference of Catholic Bishops incurred a deficit of $2 million and had to make cuts in its 1971 budget.

The decline is certainly not true of all denominations, especially in some of the smaller conservative groups such as the Assemblies of God, who opened 210 new churches in 1971 and 1,578 in the last 10 years.[14] But again, one of the big stories of 1972 was the continued decline of most major denominations in reported income and membership. The 1972 figures reveal that the second largest U.S. Protestant denomination, The United Methodist Church, recorded its fifth straight year of a membership loss.[15] Although the largest Protestant body, the Southern Baptist Convention, increased slightly in membership during the past few years, 6,000 of their churches did not record a single baptism in 1971.[16]

Needless to say, the downward trend is increasingly becoming more noticeable. *Christianity Today* says, "Church membership is no longer keeping pace with the population growth in the U.S. and church attendance is dropping off. Construction of new churches is also on the decline."

Reviewing some of the events which have contributed to this, the periodical asserts:

> The institutional church took its bumps from those inside and outside it. Jesus Freaks, renewal groups, and assorted crusaders accused the organized church of irrelevance, racism, paternalism, and repression. Most agree that structures badly need an overhaul.
>
> Shifting moral attitudes in the churches, especially concerning sexual behavior and abortion, made sensational headlines in 1970. The United Presbyterians, the Lutheran Church in America, and the United Church of Christ sanctioned—or approved for study—documents that appear to endorse pre- or extra-marital intercourse under some circumstances, and to advocate removal of legal penalties for the practice of homosexuality between consenting adults.[17]

The "handwriting appears to be on the wall" also in the new construction of religious buildings. Money, or the lack of it, is one of the most significant factors revealing denominational growth or decline. "Reports from 48 Protestant church bodies show that in 1969 their confirmed members gave an average of $99.68 during the year, just over 27 cents per day." [18] This is hardly in keeping with the Federal Income Tax, which has doubled for each person since 1960. The average member has not increased his giving to the cause of Christ as substantially as he was required to increase his income tax.

The Internal Revenue Service revealed that Americans who itemize their deductions gave less than 3 percent of their adjusted gross incomes to the church and charity during 1971. Below is a graph comparing the total contributions and average per member giving of 12 major denominations during 1960 and 1970. Church giving is hardly adequate when one assesses the tremendous inflationary costs since 1960.

U.S. News and World Report took its subscribers on a reading tour of the Episcopal Church Center, New York, national headquarters of the 3.3 million-member denomination. Instead of expansion, the reader views the belt-tightening effects of an offering-recession and inflation. The gleaming 10-story building was constructed eight years ago and was manned by a staff of 325 employees to oversee national programs and give direction to policies for one of America's most influential denominations. Today less than 100 employees are on the payroll. The magazine indicates visitors get off the elevator on the once-busy tenth floor, only to see a large sign with arrow pointing to "Clergy Deployment Office." Clergymen whose services have been recently terminated can get counsel and "leads" for their job-hunting.

Three floors have been made available to nonprofit enterprises; the broadcast studio is darkened, where tapes were once prepared for 410 stations. The reporters describe unopened mail stacked on unoccupied desks that lurk in semi-darkness. "Remaining employees, in twos or threes, work in silence, broken only by the occasional ring of a telephone or the scrape of a chair." [20]

The WASP Has a Sting

Why the cut-back at denominational headquarters? Denominational officials are usually blinded to their highhanded tactics. Rather than servicing the people, they have run roughshod over the values of their members. Mainline denominations have stuffed ghettos and black nationalism down the throats of middle-class America. The Presbyterian Church in the U.S.A. stated in

TABLE 1

TOTAL CONTRIBUTIONS AND AVERAGE PER-MEMBER GIVING DURING 1960 AND 1970

Denomination	Year of 1960		Year of 1970	
	Total Contributions	Avg/Per Member	Total Contributions	Avg/Per Member
American Baptist Convention	74,877,699	48.52	132,323,701	89.86
American Lutheran Church	50,163,078	73.52	177,018,350	69.60
Christian Church (Dis. of Christ)	84,375,152	60.93	116,057,724	81.47
Church of the Brethren	12,143,983	65.27	19,219,514	105.25
Lutheran Church in America	114,458,260	68.29	211,914,250	68.21
Lutheran Church-Missouri Synod	142,565,356	93.89	241,162,986	86.48
The Presbyterian Church in the U.S.	88,404,631	99.42	138,621,698	144.67
Reformed Church in America	22,970,935	103.23	39,414,784	103.86
Southern Baptist Convention	453,338,720	53.88	891,991,302	76.71
United Church of Christ	100,938,267	71.12	800,425,000	75.00
The United Presbyterian Church in U.S.A.	259,679,057	82.30	357,091,885	115.63
Wisconsin Evang. Lutheran Synod	14,586,801	63.05	29,393,157	77.08

1967 that peace should be sought, even at the expense of national security. Can anyone imagine that the typical Presbyterian would subscribe to such a plank? Like babies who spit up, churchmen are finding out that WASP has a sting.[21]

Many churchmen will not accept theological reasons for their problems. Bishop Roger Blanchard of Cincinnati, executive vice-president of the Church's Executive Council, agrees with the above, but also adds, "Recession is part of the story. Church pledges and contributions are the easiest place to start cutting down personal expenditures and many people have done so as their financial problems increased." [22]

The U.S. Chamber of Commerce points out that each man, woman, and child gave for all purposes an estimated $1,175 in 1970, almost double the per-capita figure of $628 in 1960.[23] However, the average contribution in these 12 religious bodies increased less than $30 per member from 1960 to 1970 ($65.28 in 1960 to $91.15 in 1970).

Another evidence that the Church is in trouble is the growing number of church buildings used for other than original purposes. In rural areas church buildings stand deserted or families live there. In the city former cathedrals are truck terminals, bars or funeral homes.

Not only are church buildings suffering de-conversion, fewer churches are constructing new facilities. The most noticeable picture that fewer church buildings are going up is seen in the 1972 *Yearbook of American Churches*:

> Estimates of the annual value of new construction of religious buildings, 1925–1970 inclusive, indicate that there was a downward turn in 1966 from the all-time high reported in 1965. This downward trend is continuing, according to 1970 estimates prepared by the U. S. Department of Commerce.[23]

Even though churches are spending less money, they are getting even smaller buildings for what they previously spent because of inflation. Construction costs have risen to such an extent that $580,230,000 in 1965 would have been sufficient to equal the $921,000,000 spent in 1970.

TABLE 2
VALUE OF NEW CONSTRUCTION OF
RELIGIOUS BUILDINGS

Year		Year	
1925	$165,000,000	1960	$1,016,000,000
1930	135,000,000	1965	1,207,000,000
1935	28,000,000	1966	1,164,000,000
1940	59,000,000	1967	1,093,000,000
1945	26,000,000	1968	1,038,000,000
1950	409,000,000	1969	949,000,000
1955	736,000,000	1970	921,000,000

Construction of new church buildings reached its height in 1965 after a tremendous boom in the 1950's. Along with the financial strain has come an anti-building mood. Liberal theologians imply that churches should put less money into buildings and more money into social programs. Churchmen have attacked the desire to construct buildings with the label "edifice complex." Gibson Winter, in his book *The Suburban Captivity of the Churches*, stated that the desire to construct large church buildings creates priority on status rather than worship.

One editorial stated:

> The anti-building mood probably got its start from the new priority given to social action by religious liberals. They urged that money be diverted from building funds to efforts to bring about needed social change.[25]

The editorial further states that factors such as the Jesus People, the charismatic movements, extravagantly overbuilt churches, and denominational or competitive pride have facilitated this feeling. But if churches don't construct buildings to gather people, there will not be a constituency from whom to collect money for social programs, staff headquarters or open the doors of theological seminaries. Then liberal professors will not have a platform to advocate their anti-institutional bias. One would accuse them of carnivorism. A danger exists in losing the gathered strength of a specific geographical base by which carefully coordinated strategy, fellowship, and outreach is launched. The editorial quips,

"Church buildings: who needs them? Christians need them to carry out the Great Commission!"

Regardless of the exact reasons for the decline of new buildings, the glaring obvious fact is a lack of interest in institutionalized religion. In all probability the decline in religion's influence, membership, attendance, and finances have all contributed to this anti-building mood, causing a snowball effect.

On the international level, the missionary outreach is another expression of denominational decline in America. While the world population has exploded to over four billion people, the missionary strength of many of the mainline denominations has dwindled in the past 15 years. The 1971 statistics for six large denominations reveal the drastic cut-back of nearly one-third of the 1958 figures.

Overseas task force	1958	1971
American Baptist Convention	407	290
United Presbyterian Church U.S.A.	1,293	810
Presbyterian Church U.S.	504	391
United Methodist Church (incl. E.U.B.).	1,453	1,175
Episcopal Church	395	138
United Church of Christ	496	356
	4,548	3,160

Dr. David Stone, a top missions executive for the United Church Board for World Ministries, noted a 10 percent decrease in missionary personnel of major U.S. Protestant denominations in the last three years. "Meanwhile, the fundamentalists and Pentecostals increased their numbers at about the same rate as the mainline churches decreased." [27]

Theology also is a cause in the missionary decline of these mainline denominations; there has been a reorientation of priorities. Instead of evangelism, these denominations laid more stress on changing the world's cultural and economic environment.

As one world-missionary strategist put it, "All the evidences we have are that this sixth modern missionary movement is *running out of steam*. It's true we're in almost every country of the world—but barely—*mere beachheads*. This is no time to quit—to let the torch drop!" [28]

Hendrik Hart summed up the problem:

> The real problem is this: the church is indeed the most important institution in the Christian community. It is so centrally important that without it there can be no powerfully effective Christian movement of any kind. However, the importance of the church lies first of all in its calling, its norm. The Head of the church and its Word never fail. But the body and its response do.
>
> Criticism makes it uncomfortable; it feels comfortable only in maintaining its rules, procedures, styles, structures, programs, traditions, heritages, and whatever else serves to keep the machine well oiled; but it is incapable of carrying on the business of the Gospel. This church considers itself to be unsinkable because of its own strength. This church finds it unthinkable that it has died and even more unthinkable that the Gospel might be radical. In contrast, only that church is unsinkable which knows itself to be a weak little ship, but which has the Master on board.[29]

Perhaps denominations today need to take an honest look at themselves, just as the Latin American Mission did in the 1950's. They examined their own decline, as compared to the explosive growth of such movements as those of the Communists, Pentecostals, and Jehovah's Witnesses. Their conclusion given in a concise statement called "the Strachaen theorem" said, "The successful expansion of any movement is in direct proportion to its success in mobilizing and occupying its total membership in constant propagation of its beliefs."[30] Its beliefs were fundamental Christianity and obedience to the Great Commission.

Possibly, lack of New Testament belief is the cause for the decline of denominational missionary outreach. Organizational machinery, social reform, contemporary relevance, and the new morality obviously are not the answers.

CONCLUSION

The mainline denominations are declining, according to opinion polls, financial records, membership rolls, church attendance statistics, and foreign mission reports. The reasons for their downward trend will be examined in the next chapters.

The American church is a complex mixture of religious dogmas, social mores, educational practices, moral prohibitions, human interrelationships, personal desires and existential identity-locus organization. Therefore, no superficial attack will be mounted. There are many causes why the future of denominations is dark. Each cause is weighed differently in its impact on the church.

This volume suggests the following reasons for the decline of denominations: (1) The disappearance of doctrinal differences, (2) the growth of mobility and anonymity, (3) lay resistance to denominational highhandedness, (4) God did not originally plan denominations. (5) the growth of secularism, (6) the growth of bureaucracy, (7) the emergence of churches that provide for all their needs apart from denominations.

NOTES

1. Constant H. Jacquet, Jr., ed., "Statistical and Historical Section," *Yearbook of American Churches,* Thirty-ninth Annual by the National Council of Churches, (New York: Council Press, 1971), pp. 223–224.
2. *Ibid.,* p. 223.
3. *Ibid.*
4. *Ibid.,* p. 224.
5. Gallup Opinion Index, *Religion in America 1971,* Report No. 70, p. 46.
6. *Ibid.,* pp. 51–52.
7. John A. Olthuis, "The Wages of Change," in *Out of Concern for the Church,* (Toronto: Wedge Publishing Foundation, 1970), p. 9.
8. *Ibid.,* p. 16.
9. Annual Gallup Audit, *The Gallup Poll,* Dec, 24, 1972, para. 6.
10. "Religion in Transit," *Christianity Today,* XVI, No. 23 (1972), p. 46.
11. W. Hewlett Stith, ed., "Editor's Notebook," *Virginia Advocate,* Vol. 141, No. 4 (1973), pp. 2–5.
12. *Ibid.,* "Conference Membership Drops," pp. 3–5.
13. "Membership Plateaus," *Christianity Today,* XV, No. 13 (1971), p. 36.
14. "Religion in Transit," *Christianity Today,* XVI, No. 7 (1972), p. 46.

15. "Religion on the Big Board," *Christianity Today*, XV, No. 7 (1971), p. 26.

16. There were more baptisms by Southern Baptists in 1971 than in any other year in the denomination's history except 1959; more than 412,000 were reported last year. However, approximately one out of six churches in the S.B.C. did not baptize anyone.

17. "Religion on the Big Board," *Christianity Today*, XV, No. 7 (1971), p. 27.

18. "Keeping Uncle Sam Afloat," *Christianity Today*, XV, No. 13 (1971), p. 27.

19. Compiled from the "Statistical and Historical Section" of the 1962 and 1972 Annual issues of *Yearbook of American Churches*.

20. "Money Squeeze Tightens in U.S. Churches," *U.S. News and World Report*, Vol. LXX, No. 6 (1971), p. 43.

21. Arthur Herzog, *The Church Trap* (New York: Macmillan Company, 1968), p. 95.

22. "Money Squeeze Tightens in U.S. Churches," *op. cit.* p. 43.

23. "Keeping Uncle Sam Afloat," *Christianity Today*, XV, No. 13 (1971), p. 27.

24. Constant H. Jacquet Jr., ed., "Statistical and Historical Section," *Yearbook of American Churches*, Fortieth Annual by the National Council of Churches, (New York: Abingdon Press, 1972), p. 260.

25. "Church Buildings: Who Needs Them?", *Christianity Today*, XVI, No. 25 (1972), p. 34.

26. "Missionary Retreat," *Christianity Today*, XVI, No. 4 (1971), p. 26.

27. *Ibid.*

28. Waldron Scott, "World Vision - God's Plan," sermon preached at the Navigator Congress on Disciplemaking, San Antonio, Texas, Dec. 30, 1972.

29. Hendrik Hart, "The Gospel is Radical," in *Out of Concern for the Church* (Toronto: Wedge Publishing Foundation, 1970), pp. 34–35.

30. Richard Peace, *Witness* (Grand Rapids: Zondervan Publishing House, 1971), pp. 35–36.

CHAPTER 3

When Distinctives Die

The Sunday morning service varies from street to street and town to town. One church reminds you of an eighteenth-century ritual, while across town you enter a "mod" church service that is free-wheeling, relevant and contemporary.

Churches meet in humble frame buildings on dirt streets, to the cathedrals with soaring spires and magnificent stained glass windows. Some churches are the "do it yourself" variety, with lay preachers and simple religious forms. Other churches are traditional American. Emerging groups emphasize "do your own thing."

Religious intensity varies from apathy in the traditional mainline denominational churches to the revivalistic fervor in fundamentalist churches. The not-so-traditional ethnic sect (Mennonite) has family tradition; and the ritualistic liturgical cathedral demands reverence from its worshippers. Those who worship in structured, loose-knit living room churches center their religious expression around Koinonia fellowship, while the emotional Pentecostal churches give members their weekly "high"; the mystical Eastern churches demand meditation and reflective worship. The only thing we know for sure is that churches are different from one another.

The American Image

American churches give many images to the worshippers. Some churches appear to follow the New England Puritan tradition: a few hymns, some praying, and finally a sermon.

47

Other churches resemble a schoolroom. The sermon-lecture is filled with references to the original text; the mind is filled with Scripture.

Moving on to the next church we find the sermon sounding like a black-racist at an anti-white rally in Harlem.

The next church visited gives the atmosphere of a group dynamics therapy session and the minister is the psychiatrist.

Everything and anything is pawned off on the American people in the name of *church*.

The difference in churches is deeper than doctrinal distinctives of denominations. There are varied reasons for the mind-boggling number of churches and denominations in America. The purpose of this volume is not to examine the differences but to determine the causes for denominational deterioration.

Denomination the Divine

When viewing the American Protestant denominational scene, their diversity and extensiveness almost defies description. Some have even indicated that to describe Protestant denominations is like trying to describe the United States—the task is too large and all-inclusive. There are over 250 denominations, some large, such as the Southern Baptist Convention with over 11 million membership; other denominations are small, such as the Two-Seeds-in-the-Spirit Predestinarian Baptists, with 201 members in 16 churches. This book cannot concern itself with every small gathering that calls itself a church or denomination. Those denominations that are considered mainline concern us; they appear as old men, aging and fossilizing.

John Hardon in his book *The Protestant Churches of America,* classified denominations and dealt with the 14 largest divisions because:

> The 14 churches in the first class were chosen on the basis of their size or because of their recognized influence in American sectarian life. They include every denomination with a half-million or more members, and the smaller groups like the Unitarian and Quakers because of their historic impact on our pluralistic society. By actual count, these 14

bodies represent 90 percent of the total Protestant affiliation in the United States.[1]

Hardon goes on to indicate that American denominations are different from other religious bodies around the world and when viewing the denominations, they are about as impossible to classify as a forest of trees.

Definition of a Denomination

When one thinks of a denomination, he usually names a group such as Presbyterian, Nazarene or Assembly of God. These historic titles do not help one understand a denomination, only to divide and classify them. There are certain characteristics that are found in denominations. These points help to limit and designate a denomination. The following technical definition will give guidance and will become the basis of discussion of religious groups for this book:

> A denomination is a group of churches with similar doctrinal beliefs, who have similar traditions and backgrounds, who share the same goals in ministry, who desire fellowship to encourage one another, and have organically bound themselves together to establish corporately what they feel cannot be wrought separately.

The above description of a denomination becomes much more inclusive than some religious bodies are willing to admit. The Southern Baptist Convention is incorporated under the above definition and is a denomination, even though many Southern Baptist pastors are appalled at the thought of such a label. To them, the tag *denomination* is a slur against their integrity. However, this is a *functional definition*.

Other groups also would bitterly oppose the label *denomination*. Groups such as the Baptist Bible Fellowship, the Christian and Missionary Alliance, the Independent Fundamental Churches of America, and the Conservative Baptist Association all fit the above definition. In chapter 7, the sociological cycle is explained and a correlation is made between theological liberalism and the sociological designation *denomination*. The above-named groups do not have liberal theology, therefore they are opposed to being called *denominations*.

Some denominations are much more centralized, while others appear to be a confederacy or unorganized fellowship. The longer a denomination exists, bureaucracy grows within the system, hence becoming a *tight denomination*. At the same time, newly emerging denominations are held together by fellowship or the fact that their churches have similar purposes. These denominations do not require a yearly report of attendance and budgets, nor do they have a district superintendent to supervise the churches. There is little centralized direction, hence little control over the individual churches. These are called *loose denominations*.

Denominations have not always been a liability to the cause of Christ. Some of the greatest revivals in America grew out of denominational cooperation for city-wide crusades such as those by D. L. Moody, Billy Sunday and Gypsy Smith. Other crusades were held when Baptists and Presbyterians gathered with other churches to reach their community for Christ. As we view the history of denominations in America, there would have been little foreign missionary outreach without denominations; individual churches did not have resources or initiative to send missionaries abroad.

If there had been no denominations, many Christian colleges would not have been built and thousands of young people would not have received training in the Word of God. There was a day when the YMCA and the YWCA made great contributions to the cause of Christ; these organizations, along with rescue missions, hospitals, social work and other humanitarian projects, were the result of denominations banded together to do corporately what could not have been done individually.

Contributions of the Denominations

The great Sunday School movement the last part of the nineteenth century resulted from denominational willingness to encourage one another to teach children the Word of God. According to Noel Smith, editor of *Baptist Bible Tribune,* "If you take denominations out of the United States, you would have little Christianity left." Smith is quick to add, "It seems that the day of the denomination is past." He went on to indicate that "Protestantism has had its day; they bore a protest against the Catholic church." Smith sees the day of denominations and protestantism declining and the answer to Christianity in America as the true New Testament church.

We should be quick to add that, even though denominations are different, they are not necessarily hostile to each other. Most who make up their churches realize they hold much in common with other churches. When the mainline denominations were more orthodox than today, they had similar views about the Scriptures. Even though there was a distinction in beliefs, Jesus Christ was the underlying catalyst. While some denominations differed in beliefs, others differed in church practices and structure. While unity did exist among many denominations, there were certain differences sufficient enough to cause people to maintain separate organization and offices. In the past, as in the present, most Christians realize these differences strengthen all groups and broaden the outreach into more communities, hence there was little strife among denominational people.

Since denominations, which are built on doctrinal differences, exist only when there is a need for different doctrine; it was only inevitable that denominations would decline with the growing de-emphasis on doctrine and increasing harmony among all Christians.

Built by Conflict

Denominations grew when their church leaders were confronted with a situation which required a theological struggle for the right of existence. The Baptists had to immerse new Christians in obedience to their understanding of Scripture, just as the Wesleyans had to seek sanctification because they believed in eradication. These groups not only justified their practice but had to marshal their defense against opposing views. If a Christian couldn't answer an opposing view, then he had to espouse it.

But the progress of democracy worked silently and inexorably toward disintegrating the forms that had brought difference into existence. It is not so much that leaders have stopped believing their distinctives, but secularism (see chapter 6) has eroded the foundations of authority. Creeds have become irrelevant in our action-oriented churches. Time was on the side of doctrinal deterioration. Denominational growth was on the side of division. When divided loyalties were diminished, the day of denominations began to ebb.

Americans drifted away from mainline denominational churches, evidenced by declining membership, decreasing attendance, and smaller financial offerings. At first, religious observers tried to explain away the drift by saying, "The post-war religious boom is over and churches are leveling off." They observed an upsurge in religion after every major war; this had happened after World War II. They argued the decline in attendance, membership, and offerings was only a return to normalcy. A second reason suggested that denominations were "paring their rolls." One denominational official indicated they were simply cleaning dead wood from their rolls; church attendance had always been stable, along with membership. They argued the decline was simply a paper statistic, not a reality on Sunday morning. But there were other disturbing signs. The decline in offerings was a reality that could not be explained away. When a denomination had to trim budgets, drop excess personnel and borrow money to meet operating expenses, evidence of a greater story was brewing.

Liberal Theology

One of the basic causes for the death of denominations is liberal theology, which sows the seeds of self-destruction: i.e., liberalism denies the strong corporate church community, with its implied authority, discipline and clear objective goals. Liberalism denies the church that gave birth to its existence. Liberalism is the grown child turned cannibal, who feeds off the corpse of its parent.

Churches and denominations are built on voluntary membership. Most individuals join the church of their choice, even though there are external forces which motivate them to membership. These external forces may be a strong pulpit presentation, denominational magazines, tracts, radio and/or telecast, personal evangelism, or the family altar. The child born to religious parents is exposed to the church's teaching. He doesn't have the privilege to stop attending the church. The parents have many years of influence over the child, to "condition" him into church membership.

Voluntary choice of a church is usually bound with personal salvation. Members attend church because of the obligation of salvation. Other people join churches because of informal pressure to conform to community life, while others join for status reasons. Whatever the reason for joining, after becoming a member, the frequency of attendance, the amount of financial giving and the intensity of adherence to theology and the purpose of the church, are the individual's own decisions. When a member strongly objects to the way his church is going, he is free to join another church or to withdraw completely from church attendance. If he doesn't like the minister or he disapproves of the way the money is spent, he can stop giving and register a vocal or silent protest. If the member objects violently, he usually stops attending altogether. In a few cases, one individual is able to organize a small corps who are able to reverse decisions, fire pastors and disassociate churches from denominations and/or the National Council of Churches.

The term "voluntary association" must be examined. When an individual voluntarily associates himself with a church, he in a broad sense accepts the church's aims. There is usually some personal satisfaction or benefit which motivates the individual to continue his association. This benefit may be of a secondary nature or even in his subconscious. Hadden gives the following illustration:

> Thus, for example, a member of a bridge club may not be a patticularly good bridge player and as such may not derive a great deal of satisfaction from playing bridge. However, the ongoing satisfaction of sociability with a group of friends may be more than adequate reward to sustain membership in the group. When a person who does not play bridge well ceases to enjoy the company of other players, there is little reason to continue membership in the group and the chances are pretty great that this person will drop out. The point is simply this: a person who derives nothing from participating in a voluntary association is not likely to continue to participate. Similarly, if the negative factors involved in partic-

ipating are perceived to outweigh the positive benefits, membership, or at least commitment, is likely to be curtailed.[2]

When the aims of a local church are changed, the leader must make sure that the membership accepts the new aims, because dissatisfied members will drop out. Otherwise the leader must recruit new members who share his aims of the church. If the leader fails to recruit those of like aims, his church will decrease in attendance, membership and offerings. This is exactly what has happened among mainline denominations. The president of a Midwest bank who was a member of a United Methodist Church indicated, "I go to church to hear about God, because I know I am a sinner . . . because I need forgiveness of my sins . . . I need to be motivated to pray. But all my minister ever talks about are the problems of the city, the blacks and the Communists." The bank president changed his membership out of a feeling of alienation from the local Methodist church.

The minister of a Protestant church has a greater precariousness than leaders who have "captive members." In the business world, employees take a shift in the company's direction for monetary reasons; they accept new aims or get fired. In the army, a shift of objectives becomes fairly easy to implement because the soldier has a three-year hitch. However, the Protestant minister must operate within boundaries of the will of his people. When he deviates beyond the congregation's desire, he is inviting disaster and/or deterioration.

Questioning Authority

Historically, church members in America have not seriously objected to their ministers. But now, the slow erosion of membership and financial contribution may take one of two directions. First, that protest which began as a trickle may grow into a raging mountain stream. Many laymen who have entrusted their denomination's authority to professional leaders seriously doubt how the authority is being used. More laymen shall begin questioning denominational policy at the annual meetings. Some mainline denominations may have a revolution on hand. A second trend may be complacency. The past trend may continue in the future.

When the average suburbanite father disagrees with his church he will slowly drift out of its influence. He will get in his camper, drive to his second home on the lake or he will sleep in on Sunday morning.

The annual budget of many mainline denominational churches has been dipping and will probably continue in the same downward pattern. Even though many denominations have endowments, wills, a rich portfolio or are underwritten by foundation funds, most of them cannot continue without voluntary contributions of their members. Within a matter of time the mainline denominational churches will lack that for which they were originally incorporated—people.

In Chicago, a manufacturer withheld a $250,000 pledge to McCormick Theological Seminary because of his objections to the church's involvement in civil rights. He gave the money to an evangelical seminary. A Negro minister in an all-white congregation in Washington, D.C., was met with resistance, resulting in a 50 percent decline in attendance and offering. The officers of the United Presbyterian Church of America persisted in donating money to defend Angela Davis, charged with conspiracy in the death of a courtroom judge. According to an opinion poll, the church members were opposed to the denominational support of Miss Davis but the officials ignored their obligation to the clientele of the denomination. It is difficult to determine how many similar incidents have brought about membership rebellion against the local church and denomination. However, the rebellion by the masses probably has been greater than has been reported.

Two Great Scandals

The mainline denominational ministers have been drifting toward liberalism at an astonishing rate, but it took two glaring examples to shock the average member out of complacency. First, was the "God is dead" movement, which was opposed by a vast majority of laymen. Second, statistics revealed skepticism among the ranks of the clergy. Glock and Stark indicated that 29 percent of six Protestant denominations had some doubts about the existence of God, 43 percent doubted that Jesus was born of a virgin and 35 percent were skeptical about life after death. When it came to believing in the authority and inspiration of the Bible, only 13 percent of Methodist ministers agreed, 5 percent of the Episcopalians, 12 percent of the Presbyterians and 33 percent of American Baptists. Almost the same statistics reflected acceptance of the creation story as literally true.[3]

Most church professionals argue that their rejection of orthodox doctrine does not necessarily represent the cause for deteriorations of denominations. Even though a causal relationship cannot be proved, there is correlation that when liberalism has grown, religious vitality has decreased.

CONCLUSION

The erosion in denominations is serious, but if attention is given immediately the trend can be reversed. When a farmer's field begins to wash away, immediate reaction saves the topsoil. If he procrastinates, the whole hillside can wash away and he can lose his source of income. Denominational strength is beginning to ebb and mainline churches are staring bleakly into the senior-citizen years. Attendance *is* going down, but what of the future? The prospects are for a snowballing effect, with greater attrition in the last half of this decade than in the early 70's. At present we find the number of ministerial candidates drying up. Churches are being closed. Budgets are being cut back, hence the work of denominations is shrinking, rather than expanding. These danger flags point to a downhill spiral.

Denominations are dying, when many other American institutions are struggling for existence. The invention of the automobile has struck mass transportation in its Achilles' heel. The advent of the public school bus has almost eliminated the one-room country school. The growth of violence in our streets has bankrupted many businesses in the downtown areas. Home television has darkened many movie houses. America is experiencing change, leading to the decay of its institutions. Mainline churches with archaic programs and dead Christianity may also be cleared by sociological bulldozers.

As the thermometer goes down, there are chilly days ahead. The decline will intensify.

NOTES

1. John Hardon, *The Protestant Churches of America* (Garden City, New York: Image Books, 1969), p. 17.

2. Jeffrey K. Hadden, *The Gathering Storm in the Churches* (Garden City, New York: Doubleday & Company, 1969), p. 28.

3. Charles Y. Glock and Rodney Stark, *Religion and Society in Tension* (Chicago: Rand McNally & Company, 1965), pp. 117–118.

CHAPTER 4

Is God Responsible for Denominations?

Immediately following the days of Pentecost, the church was a visible force in the community. The apostles had one message, Jesus Christ and Him crucified. The Church was neither a political nor an ecclesiastical organization. Preaching concerned itself with preparing people to live with God in another world. The Church was a religious association, formless and nameless, at first composed wholly of Jews; only later were Gentiles admitted into the body of Christ.

Seeds of denominationalism were found early in the book of Acts; two great churches evolved, each a little different from the other. First, there was a Jewish church at Jerusalem; its members met on Solomon's porch, they had all things in common and banded together to saturate the Holy City. We read of these Christians, "daily in the temple and every house, they ceased not to teach and preach Jesus Christ" (Acts 5:42). The Jerusalem church grew and was numbered in the thousands (Acts 2:41; 4:4; 6:1,7). Next, a great church evolved to the north, outside of the Holy Land, a Gentile church at Antioch. Their members were first called "Christians." The church had spiritually gifted leaders, Barnabas and Paul. We read of this Gentile church, "much people was added unto the Lord" (Acts 11:24). They assembled themselves together and taught much people throughout Antioch. The Gentile church was more world-mission-minded than was the Jewish church, and sent Paul and Barnabas out as the first missionaries (Acts 13:1–3).

The seeds of dissension were inherent in the nature of these two churches and were reflected into controversy at the council at

Jerusalem. The first issue to divide Christendom was circumcision, the Jewish church demanding "except ye be circumcised after the manner of Moses ye cannot be saved" (Acts 15:1), whereas Gentile churches held views similar to the conclusion of the council, that circumcision was not necessary.

The leaders of the churches were called to Jerusalem for a conference, including Peter, Paul, James and others. The problem was stated and leaders were given opportunity to state their opinion. After a lengthy discussion a group concensus was reached: "Then pleased it the apostles and the elders, with the whole church" (v. 22). The group had to work out their differences for continued fellowship. "It seemed good unto us, being assembled with one accord" (v. 25). The problem among individual churches was solved by a mass meeting, giving a biblical basis for church meetings (councils, committees, or conferences) to solve their problems. The conclusion was "For it seemed good to the Holy Ghost, and to us, to lay upon you no greater burden than these necessary things: That ye abstain from meats offered to idols, and from blood, and from things strangled, and from fornication: from which if ye keep yourselves, ye shall do well. Fare ye well" (Acts 15:28,29). Even though the churches met for a decision, there was no pressure from an authoritarian head or centralized government. Even the answer was not a command to the church at Antioch, nor did any of the apostles attempt to exercise lordship over an individual church. At the core of the Jerusalem Council was a recognition of the importance of the local church, rather than a doctrine of denominationalism; each church was autonomous. The will of the majority was not forced on any individual church.

Two Great Churches

Two great churches, both blessed of God, yet different in their interpretation of the Christian life. Whereas later denominations differed over doctrine, these first two churches differed over practice. After the council, the churches agreed to exist and minister through their separate ways, yet stay in fellowship.

We might consider what damage could have been done for the cause of Christ if "American denominationalism" had been perpetrated on the Mediterranean world in the first century. Can we think of foreign missionaries going into Corinth, one building a Jewish church with allegiance to Jerusalem, and a second Gentile church with allegiance to Antioch? The cause of Christ would have been done irreparable harm.

But what God did not allow in the first century, He permitted in these last centuries. It is the thesis of this book that God never intended denominationalism to grow into its present splintered form, so that in one city over 100 different denominational churches are found. Even though God's primary purpose was not the establishment of denominational churches, He blesses churches of various denominations, even when some churches hold minor unbiblical beliefs. When a church's strengths are greater than its weaknesses, the gospel can have some effect. Hence the message can go farther and deeper because churches exist with different emphases and practices.

Later in the book of Acts the Christians at Jerusalem were going through a famine. Paul took up an offering from the Corinthian Christians to help them in this matter (II Cor. 8:9). Once again there was no control or central treasury. One church simply provided help for another.

The book of Acts ends with a number of individual churches, each having fellowship with the other, yet no centralized superstructure is emerging. Paul, wrote from his imprisonment at Rome, the book of Acts is unfinished, indicating that the church which had begun should continue in its original form. At the apostle's death, the only common denominator among the churches was salvation predicted in the Old Testament and fulfilled in the Person of Jesus Christ, who was dead yet now lived at the right hand of God the Father. Churches seemed to recognize one another, receive gifts from one another, and transfer members from one church to another. An attitude of love characterized Christians as they helped one another in their service to Jesus Christ.

Beliefs Are Written Down

After the post-apostolic age, the church began to express its beliefs and practices on paper. The living fellowship of the church was reflected in creeds and statements of expectation. The *Did-*

ache and other doctrinal creeds inevitably appeared. Intellectual conformity to the emerging creeds was the way a Christian expressed his heart's dedication. The creed-makers fought life-and-death struggles in those early days for the deity of Christ. Eventually Christians had to fight theological battles for all other major church doctrines. When a person did not conform, he was threatened with excommunication. Personal infidelity was equally rewarded. The church grew within the Greek-intellectual milieu. Some of the greatest scholars of this time were located within the church, rather than outside its walls.

During the third century, Christianity was announced as an official religion of the empire. When the hordes of barbarians demolished the outward forms of the already decayed Roman Empire, the only remaining nucleus of social order was the preachers of the gospel who garbed themselves with simple apparel and proclaimed faith in a living God. Church control over society grew; denominationalism was never considered.

Centralization of Authority

In the decades after the apostles, a centralization of authority began to arise. The office of bishop (elder or pastor) began to grow in authority. Bishops no longer gave leadership to only one church; their authority extended over several churches within a geographical area. Bishops began to ordain men into the ministry and control the financial affairs of the churches. Each city had its own bishop supervising the work of smaller surrounding churches. Usually the greater the city, the greater the bishop's authority. Since Rome was the capital of the civilized world, the bishop in Rome became a leading ecclesiastical figure. As individual cities fell to the invading Huns, their bishops and churches were also destroyed. Rome was the last city to hold out against the invaders, hence Rome was the last city to have an ecclesiastical leader.

Ignorance prevailed throughout the world; the church which held the lamp of knowledge, saw the light flicker through superstitions, tradition and the addition of works to the grace which had been preached by the apostles.

The church became a church-state, a political-religious institution, and was the only organization able to compete with the times. There was unity in Christian profession and practice. The individual's life was closely controlled by the church's authority. A Christian's belief was born out of deep conviction to God and duty to his church. The problem of such a structure was that the sins of the clergy were hidden from the public and the weaknesses of the organization were not seen by the laymen. There was no criticism from without. Since all religious organizations created by fallible human beings are destined to destruction, the church began decaying. The church hid the light of the gospel under a bushel and sent the world into the Middle Ages.

It was inevitable that the conscience and reason of man should revolt from the intolerable claims of papal absolutism. Martin Luther personified that revolt and gave rise to the Lutheran church, and for the first time in history two widely accepted church systems were evident in the world: Catholicism and Lutheranism. But others also were rebelling against Rome. John Calvin laid the foundation for the Presbyterian church; Zwingli laid the grounds for Arminianism. Doctrines which had been undiscovered, forgotten or ignored now were discovered, declared and defended. Man's conscience and reason gave him access to the Word of God. He saw the light and rebelled against the darkness. Men had no problem with the glare of Truth; it was the shadows that gave him trouble.

These questionable areas were unimportant in the early days of the reformation; men were glorying in their new-found liberty of the gospel. But divisions were inevitable. Men disagreed on minor points, and the minor doctrines became major.

Sin has always been man's problem. Sin blinds man's understanding (II Cor. 4:3,4; I Cor. 2:14), so that he cannot fully and correctly know God. Sin brings on religious pride which leads to doctrinal arrogance, causing good men to disagree and divide over theological distinctives. Also, sin influences man's motives, so that he will recruit and train disciples to perpetuate his doctrinal beliefs. Usually, what is a doctrinal tangent in the founder of a movement becomes heresy in his spiritual grandchildren. They hold the doctrine more vehemently with less understanding.

How Does God React?

How does God react to doctrinal differences? One can only guess, "He that sitteth in the heavens shall laugh" (Psalm 2:4), when He sees the childish games played by denominations. Surely God cannot sanction false doctrine; baptism by sprinkling and immersion can't both be right. Therefore, one must be wrong. Yet, God seems to use sincere men on both sides of the issue. God does not bless their false teaching, but when a church preaches the gospel, God uses them to the extent that they have the truth and seek His blessing on their ministry. At the same time, some churches have the truth but are dead (in my observation). These churches accomplish nothing for eternity because they neglect spiritual power and disobey the truth they have.

God must work in this doctrinal milieu; therefore we conclude denominations are not the perfect will of God. He could never plan a church to express false teaching. Therefore, denominations exist within the permissive will of God. He condescends to use the frail creations of religious organizations.

But there are other causes that brought about denominations. The pluralistic society of America gave rise to denominations, like no other nation since Pentecost. A careful study of church history will show five or six church types developed within a country, but no nation has spawned the hundreds of denominations like the United States of America. After all is said and done, Christianity can only be divided into five or six major camps, each reflecting a doctrinal statement and each reflecting its own organization. But the United States is different: The strong individualism found in this new frontier community gave rise to a diversity of denominations. Man was free to believe what he wanted. Also, he had the liberty to start a church and, if he chose, start a denomination.

Americans Glorify Heroes

Americans glorify their heroes, such as the sheriff who walked into the frontier town and cleaned it up with his guns and fists. We have our legends of Bat Masterson, Doc Holliday, Tom Sawyer and TV's Matt Dillon. If the hero is not the frontier marshal, it's the Deerslayer or the Pathfinder, Tarzan or the Lone Ranger. The invincible man against overwhelming odds brings an unbelievable victory. Thus, Americans have produced the man of God, with a Bible in hand and faith in his heart; he walks into a town and cleans up the sin. He establishes a church. Americans admire strong biblical individualism and firm convictions. The frontier preacher establishes a church and gathers a congregation around his leadership; the stronger the leader, the larger the following. Thus great men build great churches. But the movement doesn't stop there. Strong leaders gather several around their cause, hence building a denomination.

Denominations also have grown out of social conditions. The growth of the Baptist groups in the United States reflects the independent spirit found growing among new nations. A serious schism evolved between the Baptists of the North and South in a disagreement over the slavery question. The Northern abolitionists argued from Scripture that it was inherently sinful to hold a title deed on a fellow human being. Very clearly, the enslavement of men was wrong to them. At the same time, Southern churchmen held that many blacks had come to know Christ through their contact with their white masters, and that the combined lot of the Negro was greatly improved over their former life in Africa because of American slavery. In April, 1845, the Southern slaveholding Baptists voted separation and a month later formed the Southern Baptist Convention, "a new type of Baptist organization, being a firmly centralized denominational body functioning through various boards." The Northern Baptists were left to organize their own foreign mission work, along with evangelizing those above the Mason-Dixon line. It remained the Northern Baptist Convention until a new name was adopted in 1950, the American Baptist Convention.

Freedom and Mobility

Freedom and mobility in America are also causes for denominations. We are a traveling people and, according to statistics, 20 percent of Americans change their address every year. In the old country generations lived and died in the same community, but

Americans pack their suitcases for greener pastures at the drop of a hat or whim of the sales manager who transfers young executives from one city to another.

Community stability mitigates against the growth of denominations. When families grow and die in the same community, it is difficult to get them to change church membership, much less establish new churches, leading to new denominations. Children tend to join the same church as their mother and grandparents. However, when a family moves to a new town, there is a tendency to lose moral restrictions and, with it, to drop church loyalties. Americans attend the church of their choice, which is usually the most convenient in the neighborhood or the one where the pastor's personality appeals to them. Hence, it is possible for aggressive denominations to build new churches and increase membership. Lethargic denominations tend to lose members. Americans want to go "where the action is," therefore they attend the church that has life or aggressive outreach. They want to use adjectives such as "fantastic!" "super-aggressive" or "streamlined." A mobile nation makes possible the growth of denominations, and since the United States is the most mobile nation in history, we can only expect to find a greater number of denominations in our nation than in any other since Pentecost.

CONCLUSION

The Bible teaches, "One Lord, one faith, one baptism, one God and Father of all" (Eph. 4:5,6). Yet in America we find many churches and many forms of worship. If there is "one body" (Eph. 4:4), which is the church, then all denominations can't be right. Some must be wrong. And yet many churches are faithful to a central core of fundamental doctrine. God has blessed individual churches according to their proximity to truth. This chapter asks the penetrating question, "Is God responsible for denominations?" The answer should not be shouted from city office buildings, but whispered in denominational board meetings. The answer is no!

CHAPTER 5

The Rise and Fall of Denominations

Vernon Harrison opened a hamburger stand, serving ground round-steak burgers, bigger than those of anyone else in town. His wife baked the plump buns; he personally mixed the sauce and fried the burgers greaselessly to perfection. Customers flocked into his small seven-booth restaurant. He expanded the dining room, added another grill, hired a baker—and people were still turned away at the door.

Harrison had business acumen, so he opened another restaurant across town and, to alert his clientele to the same kind of service and quality, he personally dubbed it Harrison's Hamburger House; next he copyrighted the name, "The Triple-H Drive-In." The new venture demanded an improved bookkeeping system to insure control and profits. He drove from one location to another to insure quality in the sauce, buns, preparation and service.

Joe Promotion also ran a hamburger house, but one losing money, even though he sold more hamburgers in one super-Drive-In than Harrison did in both locations. Joe Promo did it through high volume-low price, but was facing bankruptcy. The two men got together, Joe trying to pick Harrison's brains. The outcome was simple: Harrison would operate Joe Promotion's restaurant and control quality, business procedure, and customer service, for a percentage of the profit. Other businessmen heard about Harrison's success in helping floundering hamburger houses. Operations expanded among the hamburger fraternity; they all grew rich. Harrison began opening other hamburger houses.

Hamburger men had nothing to do with pizza people, chicken-fryers, or the taco crowd. They were friends but, according to them, hamburgers were the center of man's appetite; why appeal to fringe desires?

The hamburger men pooled their resources and opened a "Triple-H Drive-In" within one mile driving distance of every American. They all got rich.

Eventually Vernon Harrison had to appoint executives to supervise the growing empire. A chief baker maintained quality rolls, as did the chief cook, sauce chief, service chief and advertising chief. Tomichichi was appointed to supervise the chiefs. He was an Indian chief.

Vernon died, as did most of the original chiefs. Biscuits were substituted for rolls because the National Biscuit School said they were better. Some Triple-H Drive-Ins began offering spaghetti; a few strong-willed managers withdrew and changed their name—after all, they were hamburger houses. A few sticky lawsuits clouded the issue. Other drive-ins in the chain began offering shrimp, egg rolls and poi.

All the chiefs got together and decided lamb was cheaper than prime beef; after all, they concluded, "Every American needs some good mutton whether he wants it or not." Sales declined. Investors stopped opening new Triple H's. A few of the older stands in rural areas were merged.

The chiefs decided Chinatown needed hamburgers made out of mutton. The new venture failed; Chinese still wanted chop suey. Another chief bit the dust.

The Advantages of Denominations

When viewed as a parallel, even though a crude illustration at best, denominations are in the franchise business. Doctrinal distinctives are the primary cause for denominations, but different theology is not the only reason for separate religious bodies. Each group came into existence to meet the needs of individual Christians and local churches. Headquarters should exist to provide service to the members, their ministry reinforcing the outreach of each church where doctrinal distinctives are perpetuated.

The following listed points give systematically the advantages of a denomination. The terms *services* and *advantages* are used synonymously.

PURPOSE

1. *Education.*—One of the basic necessities of a denomination is to indoctrinate the young born into its group and teach the new converts the purposes and distinctives that have created the denomination in the first place. If the new members are not aware of the distinctives that give life to their church's existence, then the denomination will deteriorate when the second generation takes over leadership and the first generation passes out of existence. Lay education takes place primarily through Sunday School, Training Union, lay institutes. The success of the educational program depends upon the teacher and the curriculum. The average local pastor does not have time to write Sunday School literature, prepare training programs, formulate women's programs and give attention to the other literature needs of his people. A denomination can pool its resources to prepare quality programs and adequate literature. Full-time editors, mass printing, proofreaders, and up-to-date business procedures can supply better literature to each church at lower prices. A church purchases its literature from headquarters so that members may have a comprehensive coverage of denominational beliefs and practices that all members are expected to follow. Denominational literature employed by lay leaders enables all members to understand the reason for which their church exists. If a Nazarene doesn't understand why he's a Nazarene, what's wrong with his becoming a Methodist?

Content of Literature

The content of educational literature is usually arrived at by reciprocal agreement between the individual churches and denominational officials who are usually responsible for the content. The unique distinctives of the founder of a denomination give direction to a movement. John Wesley's writings, journal entries and sermons gave the impetus to the growth of the Methodist church. His unique teaching on holiness separated Methodist adherents from the Church of England and other denominations. But today the original teachings of John Wesley are not rigidly followed in the Methodist church. His views on sanctification are explained as either unacceptable for sophisticated America or his views are reinterpreted into contemporary practice. In either case, the original direction of John Wesley no longer gives guidance to the United Methodist Church. When Methodist practices and beliefs become similar to all other denominations, the question is asked, "Why should members remain Methodist?"

Denominational officials hold educational conferences to determine the content of Sunday School literature. Each time the members vote upon a new slant or contemporary interpretation, the curriculum takes new shape, hence evolving over a period of time. Southern Baptists have traditionally used literature from Convention Press, Nashville, Tennessee, because it uniquely portrays the belief of Baptists. However, there are numbers of Southern Baptists who no longer use their own literature. Marvin Kaningeiter, of Baptist Publications, Denver, Colorado, reports a growing number of Southern Baptist churches using their independent Baptist material because of its unique conservative position and historic Baptist stand.

The rebels in a denomination not using its literature are slowly educating themselves out of the denominational orbit. Also, by a silent vote they are repudiating the direction of the denomination. Should a church remain in a denomination when it cannot support its educational services?

Colleges and seminaries are another form of educational service to denominational churches. Historically, conservative churches have begun denominational colleges to educate their young, prepare ministers for full-time service, thus perpetuating their existence. Colleges are seldom begun in the decaying stage of religious bodies; they are founded in the beginning days of denominations. The author noted that large independent Baptist churches have begun over 61 colleges in the last two years. Liberals seldom have the religious dynamic and sacrifice to begin colleges; they capture them from conservatives.

The Word of God

2. *Evangelism.*—A church that gives allegiance to the Word of God is aware that Christ commands, "Go ye therefore, and teach all nations, baptizing them in the name of the Father, and of the Son, and of the Holy Ghost" (Matt. 28:19). Therefore, a Christian church should feel an obligation to witness to those within the community, as well as those in surrounding communities without a gospel witness. Then beyond its home responsibility, a church should feel an obligation to preach the gospel in foreign fields (Acts 13:1–3). A church which fulfills its evangelistic obligations usually joins hands with other churches in a program of establishing branch churches or Sunday School missions. Teams of workers are sent to teach Sunday School, lead singing and administer branch churches. When surrounding cities need a gospel witness, an individual church can help financially to set up a home missionary to begin a church.

It is only natural that when finances are given to help establish a new church, it will be similar to the one which gives the finances. Since a church should be a careful steward of its finances, it should make sure that new churches are similar in doctrine and purpose. Sometimes a new church changes direction or changes theology. Then all of the financial outlay will go to a cause that does not support the gospel. Therefore it is only natural that some central control is necessary when new churches are established. This control is simply setting standards to commission missionaries, set up church standards, and provide a revolving loan fund so an infant congregation can secure needed capital.

Validated by a Name

When an infant congregation begins in a community, the prospective member wants to know something about a church before he pledges his attendance and financial support. When the new church can identify with an existing denomination, it is easy to attract new members. The names, "Holiday Inn," or United Airlines," mean a standard of quality to most Americans. The name, "Presbyterian Church," carries a certain image and helps to attract people favorable to that image.

3. *Ministerial recognition.*—When a young man enters the ministry, he goes through the process of ordination, which is simply man's recognition of God's call and blessing upon his ministry. At an ordination service, men of like faith (from the denomination) gather to lay their hands upon the head of the young man, setting him apart to the ministry. This act of recognition gives the new minister certain access into ministerial associations, privilege to perform weddings and funerals and supervise other religious acts. For the most part, ministerial recognition is registered at denominational headquarters, except in some circles where the local church plays a prominent role.

In denominations with centralized authority, ministers are assigned to their charges by the superintendent or bishop who supervises the area. In denominations where authority resides in the local church, pulpit committees made up of lay leaders usually confer with denominational officials to find proper candidates.

Standards are set for the local parish preachers, usually by consensus vote of parish ministers and denominational officials. Usually a minister must have seminary education at the denominational seminary and, by an ordination examination, show theological proficiency and give evidence of leadership in the church.

Church standards are usually founded upon the Word of God. These are usually printed to give guidance to young men entering the ministry, as well as direction to the ministry of those already serving Christ.

The denomination furnishes other services to ministers such as: hospitalization, pension and/or retirement homes for ministers. In the past many denominations operated a home for aged ministers, in lieu of a retirement fund. Now, most ministers are treated as are other retirees in the American community. The fact that ministers are given more liberty than was evident a few years ago, is significant of the changing attitudes toward the ministry. The minister has lost some of the glow on his halo; the clergy is considered more secular than in the past.

Another Important Service

Inspiration, counsel and encouragement is another important service that the denomination gives to the local church. When the local pastor is faced with problems, he needs access to someone with whom he can counsel in his need. In former days successful pastors were elevated to the position of superintendent or bishop. These men counseled with the young pastors concerning their problems. Modern denominations have established counseling departments to specifically deal with personal problems of the young minister, in addition to technical counseling for church organizations and administration. These departments might include church architecture, financing, printing. Departments and committees commissioned by the denomination also give direction to individual churches.

The annual denominational meeting provides fellowship and inspiration to pastors and local churches. Pastors are challenged to return home and build their congregation. Inspiration and motivation, along with education and training, become another way of servicing the local congregations. The annual meeting also coordinates the work of the denomination through committees, leading to resolutions and united action.

In the past, denominational affiliation has been prized or treasured by church members. The Baptist was proud to tell everyone he had been immersed; the Presbyterian held his head erect as he told folks he was a Calvinist; the vice-president of the bank mentioned casually to a customer that he took communion at the Episcopal church. Church rituals and customs were points of personal preference and dignity. The distinctives of a denomination were valued by its members.

However, we have moved into an age where the ideological walls between denominations have evaporated. One church is no different than another. They seem to be all the same. The resulting merger of beliefs has also seen apathy in the members. The cab driver is no longer proud to tell you he attends the Methodist church, unless you too are Methodist; he then will confess to being Methodist with hopes of a larger tip. Housewives at a coffee or brunch do not talk about the differences between their churches, rather they talk about the things they have in common.

Jekyll or Hyde?

No one can measure the vast contribution that denominations have made to the United States. Only God knows the exact count of souls that have been converted because of cooperation among conservative denominational churches, even though church sur-titles were different and distinctives were minor. There are a numberless body of students who have been taught in Christian colleges founded by denominations. Hospitals have been founded, unmarried mothers helped, the homeless fed, and laws enacted in keeping with the Puritan ethic, all through denomi-national cooperation. Denominations have stood in the spotlight; God has used them to His glory.

But the nagging question remains unanswered: Did God orig-inally plan a splintered gospel outreach? This manuscript main-tains that the local church sits at the center of God's purpose and plan. God has a perfect will. But He also has a permissive will, which is the source of God's blessing upon denominations.

Even though God has allowed the quirk of denominations and has acquiesced to use them for His purpose, they still have a posi-tive place in the history of Christianity. But the issue does not end there. If denominations were not the plan of God, their presence must have brought about some detrimental results. If all the results of denominations are good, then God could have elected it; but He didn't. The denominations have splintered the work of God, have allowed the liberals to rape local churches, have introduced insipid bureaucracy into the cause of Christ and have estranged the love of Christians for Jesus Christ.

The following points systematically list the dangers of denominationalism:

1. *Christians give more loyalty to the denomination than to Christ.*—Christians are required to "love the Lord thy God with all thy heart, and with all thy soul, and with all thy mind" (Matt. 22:37). Christ is not only the center of the church and the purpose for which the church exists, Christ *is* the church

(Eph. 1:21,22). Though Christians may disagree on the belief of the church, most realize that a local congregation is organized to carry out the commands of Jesus Christ and to bring glory to Him in all things. Therefore, the rituals, symbols and programs are all designed to bring honor to Jesus Christ.

Misplaced Pride

Members of the Christian church are more proud of their baptism than they are of Christ, in whose name they were baptized. One man brags, "I am Presbyterian," while the next boasts, "I am Unitarian." This reminds the listener of Paul's admonishing the Corinthians who boasted, "I am of Paul; . . . I am of Apollos" (I Cor. 3:4).

In order to increase membership, offerings and loyal attendance, a pastor attempts to build respect for his church and denomination. The denominational name is prominently displayed on all literature and the distinctives are vigorously taught. What began as an honest attempt to build stronger Christians, slips into sectarian pride. Members give more loyalty to their church, at times going against their conscience. Very subtly, deterioration has begun to settle in the church and a dedicated membership is unaware of the shifting emphasis.

2. *The Christian's loyalty is shifted away from the local church to the denomination.*—The New Testament teaches that a Christian should be loyal to his local church with his attendance, offerings and service. The church is the only organization constituted by Christ (Matt. 16:18) and was the only organization in which Christians assembled, mentioned by name in the book of Acts. The local church was more than important in the life of Christians, it was imperative for their spiritual nurture and sustenance.

Denominationalism exists in the world which may demand more loyalty to the Presbyterian church or the Baptist church than to the local church where one attends. Pastors are required to spend time on committees, boards and councils, many times ignoring the work of their local congregation. Christian workers find themselves bogged down in trivia, rather than being about the primary purpose of the church—soul winning.

3. *The control of local churches shifts from the congregation*

to the denomination.—The strength of any denomination is in strong local churches. Yet, bureaucratic headquarters sap strength of individual churches; denominational officials become stronger and churches lose their authority. Strong local churches gather money, loyalty and attendance from members and, in the long run, will make for a strong denomination. However, the more loyalty demanded by a denomination, the weaker it becomes in the long run.

Who Owns the Property?

In some denominations the property title and buildings are deeded over to headquarters, even though the members have raised the down payment, arranged the financing and paid the loan. At present, there are conflicting court judgments whether a property belongs to the local congregation or the denomination. Some denominations do not hold the property but place restrictive clauses and binding agreements that the local congregation loses its autonomy and control over its own assets. Some church groups realize splinter factions may steal their members and assets, thus they encourage local churches to write a clause into their constitution turning the title of the property back to the parent body should the church ever dissolve its tie with the denomination.

Loss of control by churches happens in other areas. Churches cannot select their own missionaries, direct their own giving to benevolent funds or purchase their own literature. The pastor and official board are told that to enjoy full cooperation with the program, they should fully support the program. If a pastor does not send his young people to the denominational college and support it through yearly pledges, he is ostracized. He is not placed on important committees, nor is he invited to speak on denominational programs. The pressure is indirect, yet convincing, to some young pastors seeking denominational status.

The choice of a shepherd for the flock becomes another problem in denominational churches. In certain denominations the bishop or superintendent has final authority to place a minister in a church. In other denominations the superintendent can assign a pastor to a church, but the congregation holds veto power,

the right to reject those who are sent. Denominations with demo-
cratic government have a method of shipping ministers into line.
Denominational officials tell pulpit committees their candidates
should be screened. When these pulpit committees seek a refer-
ence at headquarters, candidates are not evaluated according to
their orthodoxy, but by their loyalty to the denominational
program. As a matter of fact, if a maverick candidate is too independent, wanting a church to go their own way under the leadership of the Holy Spirit, the candidate gets headquarters' condem-
nation, hence he is manipulated out of large churches into the
hinterlands. When the pulpit committee of Central Evangelical
Free Church, Minneapolis, Minnesota, asked Dr. A. T. Olson,
president of the Evangelical Free Church of America, about a
candidate, he simply said, "You wouldn't want him." The candidate was never approached, and no reason was given by Olson.

Candidates for Compromise?

4. *Christians in denominations are candidates for compromise.*
—Fully developed denominations have schools, colleges, seminaries, foreign mission boards, hospitals, orphanages and other
agencies of varying degrees of efficiency. Each denominational
organization is either close to or on the periphery of the commands of the Great Commission. The soul-winning Christian will
have no difficulty supporting the board of evangelism. However,
individual members may disagree with the commission on social
relationships, finding that the committee's standards weakened his
conscience and led him to compromise. The committee continually moves farther away from the belief of Christians in a local
church. The first attitude the Christian can take is like the employee who disagrees with his boss, saying, "I just work here—I
don't make policy." These Christians tolerate agencies within
the denomination with which they disagree. A few members
speak against the social relationship committee and in most
churches their voice is unheeded. Even if Christians can get their
local church to vote against the committee, a denomination will
seldom deny itself. It will support the committee, hence the local
church either has to drop out of the denomination or go its own
silent way. If it continues to cooperate, the local congregation

chooses to "channel its funds" away from the committee. Hence, this local church may send money to the foreign mission board or the board of evangelism, but not the social relations committee. However virtuous this action might be, directing funds amounts only to "paper loyalty." What funds they don't give to the offending committee are made up by gifts of other churches. Thus Christians are indirectly supporting groups with which they disagree.

As a result, we find individual churches and their members within a denomination, yet not supporting the total work of the denomination. With tongue in cheek they call themselves United Methodist or whatever allegiance they hold, yet compromise their convictions to some degree.

Deity of Christ Denied

We have seen the growth of liberalism, whereby the deity of Christ is denied in church circles. Even though Christ claimed to be equal with God the Father ("I and my Father are one"), theologians have negated His claim by humanizing the Bible. The purpose of the church is to carry out the command of Jesus Christ, "Go ye therefore, and teach all nations, baptizing them in the name of the Father, and of the Son, and of the Holy Ghost" (Matt. 28:19). Yet churchmen are suggesting that churches improve the conditions of the black, oppose war, recruit voters and attack slum problems. These conditions, while tragic and in need of our help, are not the target of the church.

5. *Denominationalism leads to the apostate church.*—Denominational loyalty forces the individual to surrender some of his individual rights and allegiance; at the same time his energies are funneled into a bureaucratic headquarters.

Ultimately, society is being maneuvered into a one-world government and a one-world church. Revelation 17 and 18 teaches that the Antichrist shall rule the world through a unified government and unified religion.

If the denomination speaks for the individual, then it will be easy for centralized control of the world's religions. If Antichrist can control denomination officials, it is a quick step to one centralized church.

The world control is a relative term and can be interpreted as external forces or control by internal persuasion. The individual voice speaking against the system will not be heard.

Not a Phoenix Situation

If denominations are dying, how can we predict the one-world church growing out of their ashes? The opposite seems to be the hypothetical answer: If denominations were to get stronger, they could merge into an ecumenical world church. The method by which the coming world church grows is not written in Scripture. Any turn of events in the near future could astound the reader, hence reversing the present decline. The present decline grows out of a repudiation of biblical Christianity. The coming ecumenical movement will be strengthened by forces outside of fundamental Christianity. We do not know how it will be strengthened and how it will grow. However, most Bible-believers feel the world church will grow from the roots of denominationalism.

Conclusion

Those who are members of denominations will identify with the first section of this chapter. Those who are members of independent churches will read the second half of this section and yell, "Hit 'em again, harder!" Denominations have been used of God, and our nation would be less Christian without them. But there is no "instant yesterday," and the future of God's work lies in another avenue.

CHAPTER 6

The Loss of Mystery

God is the ultimate mystery of the universe. Who is He? What is He like? Does divinity exist, or is God the psychological creation of man's need? God is a universal word, although some call Him Allah, Jehovah, Buddha, or Jesus Christ. Almost every tribe and race has a god; almost every religion has its rituals. Those who worship God abound; few deny His existence.

Those who believe in a God claim personal communion with Him; those who deny His existence claim there is no objective proof that there is a God.

The desire to know God or commune with Him seems to express a universal need among men. The Buddhist in India prays, as does the Shinto priest in Japan, reflecting the same expectation of the Moslem who climbs his minaret to seek the blessings of Allah. The desire for religious adoration seems to reside in large segments of the world's population.

The fact that so many seek God leads the observer to conclude there is a religious need within man. But this desire for God does not mean all will find God, at least find Him in the same way. Some men search for God and others are sure they find Him, resulting in many forms of religion in the world. Some of these spiritual societies are exclusive of all other bodies, while others have a high degree of tolerance. But all have deity at the center of their existence.

There are many religions, yet most seem to conflict with the others. The multiplicity of these religions leads the observer to conclude that if there is a God, He is hard to find, for so many have arrived at conflicting religious destinations. God is hard to understand; i.e., it is difficult to express in human words God's nature, His demands for salvation and how men should live to please God. That which can't be understood is mysterious, hence we say God is a mystery. Men cannot comprehend the miraculous or the supernatural, hence anything within the realm of God is mystery.

The author believes in the existence of a personal God who has revealed Himself in natural and supernatural media. The purpose of this chapter is not to prove God, but to show that when religious organizations deny the supernatural phenomenon of their belief, that religious body becomes secular. When a religion becomes secular, it loses its cause for existence, hence loses its mass following.

Man stands in the glaring rays of sunset and cannot comprehend what he sees. Man examines the small insect among the blades of grass and cannot fathom the balance of nature. Man marvels at the birth of a child and wonders at the miracle of life. Man considers the intricate balance of the human mind, and asks who designed the delicate organ. There is mystery in this universe, just as there is mystery beyond the metaphysical world. Religions have always attempted to explain the mystery of the material world in realms of immaterial existence. Mystery is the catalyst of religion and is the demand of religious questions: Who is God? What is He like? How can man approach the divine? What is the destiny of man in this life and the next? The answers to these and similar questions point man to the unknown, to the world of the supernatural.

Christ Is the Answer

Christianity takes its place along with the other religions of the world in seeking to answer these questions and explaining the mystery of the ages. Just as every religion sets forth answers, so the Christian maintains that all solutions to ultimate questions are answered in Jesus Christ. The revelation of Jesus Christ in Scripture deals with the eternal mystery. Christianity claims that all other religious teachings are spurious. "There is none other name under heaven, given among men, whereby we must be saved" (Acts 4:12), just as Christianity demands that all individuals come to God through Christ: "I am the way, the truth and the life; no man cometh unto the Father but by me" (John 14:6).

Mystery makes the Christian church different from social clubs, political organizations or any other fraternal gathering. As a stranger walks into a building called a church, he notices it looks different from other structures in town; its furniture is emblematic, as are its windows. Religious symbols are etched in stone, wood and cloth. For the unoriented, the meaning behind the church building is obscure. When listening to a sermon, he hears strange words in the vocabulary of the minister: *regeneration, faith, propitiation* and *atonement*. The minister uses "God-talk." Christians claim that a living personal God created this earth and sustains it through His personal power; God is imminently interested in every person and desires intimate fellowship with human man. God wants "saved persons" to come and abide with Him in heaven after this life is over.

However, those outside the church have a problem with Christianity. No one has ever seen God, at least with human eyes. Christianity is saturated with the ethereal. Those on the inside accept the mystery of Christianity, even though they don't completely understand it. Those on the outside don't understand and don't believe in the mystery. There exists a polarized position between the world of the supernatural and the world of the secular, and the mystery of Christianity is its other-world emphasis.

The eternal God remains incognito. He is pure, holy and separate from sin. He is hidden. He lives in heaven, a place no natural man has visited and returned from to tell his observations. Christians teach that God is everywhere present at the same time. He has all knowledge and He is all-powerful; yet to the average man on the street, God seems to allow the wicked to prosper; God seems to be reluctant to act in the affairs of men; and if God knows all things, He doesn't seem to care.

Men sin by going against the will of God. Sin sends men to eternal flaming punishment, a judgment seemingly inconsistent with man's understanding of a loving, compassionate God. To the man without the church, Christianity is a mystery. Even the member in the church can't fully understand Christianity (Isaiah

55:8,9), because man can't comprehend God. Man stands in awe as he ponders the infinitude of God. God is the ultimate enigma, even when expressed in man's finite words.

Christianity Is a Mystery

Christianity is a mystery and if the mystery is removed, there is no more Christianity. Mystery is the supernatural, and if the church loses it, man has nothing to believe; his spiritual help is gone. The thesis of this chapter is that creeping secularism within Christianity has made the church similar to the world about it, eradicating the mystery of Christianity and doing away with theological belief. Since doctrinal distinctives are the main basis for denominations, when they disappear, denominations also will disappear. Denominations existed as long as there were theological distinctives, the basis which first caused the growth of denominations.

Morrison has a four-point definition of secularism that gives a more practical insight into its influence: (1) A Protestant neglect of religious education, resulting from the total abandonment of the five-day school week to the political state. (2) The overawing effect of the brilliant achievement of science. (3) The disintegrating effect of commercialized entertainment upon morality. (4) The too-intimate identification of Christian liberalism with the liberalism of secular culture.[1]

The Liberal Erosion

This chapter will show how the infiltration of liberal theology has eroded commitment to a biblical faith. When churches were cut loose from their authoritarian mooring as found in the literal inspiration of Scripture, they drifted aimlessly, and the apex of the church's self-destruction was the recent "God is dead" movement. A group of young theologians who called themselves "Christian atheists" pushed Christianity as far as possible from its foundation when they proclaimed that God had died. This movement, led by Thomas J. Altizer of Emory University, Paul Van Buren of Temple University, and William Hamilton of Colgate Rochester Divinity School, received much more attention than its size warranted. Those who read their writings had difficulty understanding what the "death of God" theologians were saying. The average laymen in the pew reacted violently: "How can we celebrate the funeral of God?" However, these religious morticians were simply saying that the world, along with the church, had evolved into secularism, that the world should not be divided into a theological and physical reality. The radical theologians maintained the church should leave its religious fortress, abandon its mystery, and go out among the masses; the church should no longer be a religious conclave. Since the American man's life has become entirely secular, he must give up the "old-fashioned" idea of God—the old idea of God is dead. The secular theologians wanted to stop dividing the world into a horizontal life, where the upper story was reserved for the abode of God and the ground floor where man makes a living. The "God is dead" theologians indicate that the bi-level (or tri-level) universe was a religious appendage and as such should be done away; the thoughts of a transcendental God should be repudiated, as the growing child repudiates belief in Santa Claus and fairy tales. The "God is dead" theologians observed that the church was coming through its adolescent years and should put off its childish beliefs in a God who is "out there."

Civic Club Churches

The radical theologians were reflecting the post-secularization of the church and pushed Sunday morning worship toward a more humanistic approach. When the average American realized that his church was no different than a Kiwanis Club, he asked, "Why go?" Since he didn't get a meaningful answer, he stopped attending. Secularism destroyed mystery and brought "God-talk" down to human reason. The new modern minister talks very little about a personal, holy God, purity or a coming judgment. Ministers talk about voter registration, Vietnam, Women's Lib and quota rule.

By secularization we mean (1) man no longer believes in a supernatural God to whom he is responsible; (2) that our society or culture is removed from the control of the organized church or religious groups; (3) the ultimate purpose for which life is constituted is the good of man, and (4) the basis of meaningful action is by a pragmatic arrival at proper solutions to man's problems.

We have witnessed the secularization of our public schools, whereby Bible reading and prayer have been excluded from daily exercises. This secularization process is also noted in social life, so that abortion, premarital sex, pornography, homosexuality, nudity and alcoholism cannot be judged in view of absolute morality. What was formerly called sin is now condoned on a rational basis of being "socially conformable."

The consciences of Americans have been secularized. Children are conditioned by public schools, modern media and the "new morality;" as a result, the church has little control or influence on their lives. In the past, men who took the name of God in vain were conscious that it was wrong; however, the fear of God has been so rationalized that God's name is used as a swear word without guilt.

But perhaps the greatest travesty of all is the secularization of the church. God's house no longer occupies a central religious symbolic position in American life. Ministers are seldom consulted for direction in national issues. The church, like the Temple in the Old Testament, has seen its Shekinah glory cloud disappear.

While secularism was growing in the world, at the same time protestantism was divesting itself of the mystery of its beliefs. Liberal theologians were no longer claiming that God was "out there." According to Tillich, He was "the ground of our being" or the ultimate answer to identity crisis. As a result, the sky is empty of angels and heaven is only the destination of the astronauts. Hell is no longer a place of eternal fire but a swear word to be used when one loses his temper.

The Profane World

The new theologians spoke of the "disenchantment of the world," which meant that the world no longer had religious meaning but was completely profane. When the evolutionary hypothesis became a plausible theory to explain the origin of the world, the literal creation of the world by God was no longer needed to explain the mystery of cause. Rudolph Bultmann spoke of the "demythologization" of the Bible, whereby the miraculous was explained away and man was no longer the crowning glory of the universe; he was simply a historical actor on the stage of life. God was no longer the unexplainable enigma. The Christian congregation, which represents a very unusual organization of people specifically concerned about religion, began to deny the purpose that brought them together, an organization in counterposition with itself. The church became its own grave-digger.

Christians concentrate their religious activities and symbols into one institutional organism and define the rest of the world as "out there." As long as the church fought to preserve its identity from the onslaughts of the world, it remained pure and intact. However, the modern church appears as settlers within the fort, tomahawking the cavalry in the back, while the Indians were making their charge. The world could never defeat the church from the outside through all its onslaughts. Jesus had promised victory: "I will build my church and the gates of hell shall not prevail against it" (Matthew 16:18). So while external forces could not bring the church to its knees, she was betrayed from within by the hands of secular theologians. The church, much like Christ whom she represents, was betrayed from within. Modern-day Judases are still playing the traitor's role. As a result, the church is undergoing what Peter Berger calls a "crisis of credibility," which has resulted in the widespread collapse of the plausibility of traditional religious definitions of reality.[2]

Out of the Reformation grew three new branches of Christianity, in these groups the foundation for modern-day denominations. First, the Lutherans; second, the Anglicans; and thirdly, the Calvinists. Each group was built on its doctrinal distinctives and each received popular support from its surrounding social context. The growth of the three, especially Lutherans and Calvinists, was the result of a close nurturing by its members; the people felt the need for their churches. The intellectual differences among these three groups had an outworking in daily life; first, the people had a creed; second, a church order; and, finally, the people felt a new freedom in their Christianity. Up until the Reformation man would not step outside of the jurisdiction of church without fear of falling into mortal blackness and judgment.

The Second Reformation

These new Protestant denominations spread freely for over 100 years. Then a second shock-wave or internal reformation in the form of pietism began to influence all three groups. Within Lutheranism, the Moravians began to seek a meaningful life-style in strict adherence to purity of life. Within the Anglicans came the Puritans and their counterparts, the Pilgrims. Also, the Methodist movement grew out of the "Holy Club" at Oxford under the Wesleys. Calvinism was not without its pietistic influence; the first great Awakening in New England at the time of Jonathan Edwards spread among Calvinistic churches. The positive influence of pietism brought people back to purity of life, at the same time melting down the dogmatic or theological structures between groups. Creeds were not as important as holy living. The differences between new groups was not only intellectual belief; the new distinction between groups was now emotionalism, thus subjectizing Christianity. Methodism grew up within the Church of England; many of Wesley's doctrines were the same as the Anglicans, the difference being the life-style. Wesley's great cry was, "If your heart is as my heart, then take my hand." Out of his piety came a new doctrine where theology was minimized and the warm heart moved to center-stage.

Frederick Schleiermacher (1768–1834) was considered a pioneer in liberal theology with his emphasis on religious experience. His influence spread on the Continent, where dead orthodoxy was leaving a vacuum. He talked about a "feeling for the infinite," which he later expressed as faith. Whereas the pietist had de-emphasized doctrine to capture the lost feeling of holiness, he did so within orthodox doctrine. Now Schleiermacher felt that the supernatural elements of Christianity could be subjugated to personal experience. He ultimately made supernatural belief unnecessary, as human experience could be carried on without God. Some call Schleiermacher the father of liberalism.

Darwin gave a biological basis for religious liberalism. His theory of evolution allowed that the world could have been created without God by a "survival of the fittest" thesis. Evolution and orthodox Christianity locked themselves into mortal combat. The liberal theologians, armed with a new weapon—biological evolution—now had a God who lived in heaven, yet they lived in a world created by evolution. This meant they could have Jesus the Son of God, without His virgin birth and supernatural resurrection.

Kierkegaard (1813–1855) introduced a new area of experience into theology, the quest for meaning in life. Religious man was now to search for meaning or identity, rather than to desire an ultimate destiny in heaven. The mystery of the universe was turned within; man was seeking to find himself. Existentialism was a rising movement among religious liberalism.

The writings of Lenin and the Russian Revolution gave birth to Communism, which once again gave new ammunition to liberal theology. God was no longer necessary to explain the social affairs of man, nor was it necessary to believe in the divine appointment of rulers, such as "The powers that be are ordained by God" (Rom. 13:1). Liberalism was in the saddle and the church was riding unbridled toward the Golden Age of the Millennium, to be brought in by the combined efforts of many denominations, churches, and the cooperation of Christians at all levels of influence.

Effects of World War I

World War I was a great shock to liberal theology and seriously threatened Protestant liberalism. First, Protestant domination in Northern Europe waned and, next, the church lost its influence in England. The outbreak of revolutionary movements gave a heel blow to liberalism, while Karl Barth rendered liberalism a head blow by his publication of the *Commentary on the Letter to the Romans*. Barth declared that the God of mystery was out there and that man, by taking a leap into the dark, would find his Maker in a moment of crisis, called by some "neo-orthodoxy" and by others "crisis theology." A revolutionary theology for revolutionary times emerged in the form of existentialism—rationalism, along with a mixture of mystical and biblical theology, capturing the fancy of the theological world. For all of its ills, neo-orthodoxy did attempt to revive an objective tradition and introduced a church of form and creed. Neo-orthodoxy brought a hesitation in the church's slip into oblivion. Whereas liberalism had emphasized the individual, neo-orthodoxy attempted to turn man's attention back to the church. Barthianism grew in Germany, even though oppressed by Nazism and after the Second World War, when America experienced a revival of church attendance, neo-orthodoxy theology also experienced growth. The church was important, God as a Person was sought and men were sorry for their sins. Just how much salvation was found in neo-orthodoxy theology is questioned. However, the later decline of the church perhaps shows that the fruits of Barthianism spoiled after being exposed to the elements.

After World War II, Paul Tillich and Emil Bruner were American spokesmen for liberal theology, not completely agreeing with Karl Barth. Tillich became the rallying point for many young theologians who began to repudiate Karl Barth. His three volumes of *Systematic Theology* [3] laid the foundation for growth of secular theology: God was not a person but "the ground of being."

The German theologian Dietrich Bonhoeffer grew in popularity during the sixties, and his concept of "religionless Christianity" captured the fancy of the theological world. Bonhoeffer, a martyr of Adolph Hitler, lived in the seminaries of mainline denominations 30 years after his death. Out of the new theology came the "radical theology" and the phenomenon of God's death.

Bishop of Wolwich, John A. T. Robinson, published a bestseller in Britain and the United States entitled *Honest to God*,[4] which simply stated, "Our image of God must go." Robinson did not offer an original contribution to the world—he simply applied the liberal theology of Paul Tillich, Dietrich Bonhoeffer and Rudolph Bultmann to the man in the pew. Liberalism had been taught in the theological seminaries, but only the intellectual elite understood it. The once-a-week churchman didn't care about his pastor's theology, as long as he used terms such as *God . . . grace . . . heaven . . . forgiveness.* Liberalism caused no startling reaction among the pews. However, Robinson stuck the needle in the sleeping bear, and the laymen began arising out of their theological sleep. Many praised Robinson, while others questioned if an Anglican bishop who did not believe in God should continue as bishop of Woolwich.

Liberal Theology Themes

The Secular City,[5] a best-seller by Harvey Cox, recorded several liberal themes of theology. First, Cox dramatically portrayed that the world was moving towards secularism and away from dualistic world view. Cox indicated that the church's first social gathering was like the tribe in the primeval forest. Some people gathered together for protection and continuity. The early church, like *the tribe*, fought many battles against the elements for self-preservation. Later, the church symbolized the small-town mentality, where each man walked to work and experienced warm human relationships. The introduction of language and money propelled society from the tribe to *the town*. Later, the introduction of language and money pushed the church to the next stage in Cox's cycle, *the metropolis*, the large town where secularization took place. Cox gives two symbols as characteristic of the metropolis: the cloverleaf and the telephone switchboard. The cloverleaf is mobility, man able to travel great distances in short periods of time; and the switchboard is mass communication, so that great sections of the city have access to any and all information. The last step on Cox's cycle is *the megalopolis,* a secular city where all former concepts of God are gone. Secular man is free and charged with the responsibility to make the world as he desires. Man is no longer bound by traditional moral ethics and philosophical ideologies that focused his attention on the God of mystery. The God of tradition was dead; every man must now live in a secular city.

Today's theological seminaries are controlled by the "new breed of theologians," who hold in trust the minds of the young men who come to them. Many of the young theologians maintain that the church is dead and has been isolated and alienated from the mainstream of the American life. As a result, they feel that the church should be the institution to put an end to social injustice in the world. A recent study by the Episcopalians, *To Comfort and to Challenge*,[6] reinforces this challenge and maintains that the church should be more militant in social issues. These radical theologians charge that the 11 o'clock hour on Sunday morning is the most racially segregated hour in America and they flash such questions as, "What color was Jesus?" They charge that the major failure of the church is its inability to face up to the race issue.

Invasion of the Church

Secularism had been threatening the church from without. Now, the traditional church no longer interprets itself as being different from the world; the church is the world. Just as the vacuum cannot resist its environs, so the world invaded the church, with a resulting loss of membership, attendance and finances.

The virgin birth, vicarious death of Christ and His supernatural resurrection were no longer preached as the basis for salvation. Salvation is finding meaning in life; hell is what you get at work. Therefore, Americans asked, "Why attend church?" when they could stay home and watch their favorite TV show or take their families to the lakes. Since the supernatural is translated in terms of existential or psychological terminology, Americans turned to group dynamics. When personal problems arose they visited the psychiatrist's couch. Put simply, the problem of the universe was answered by evolution, the problem of sin was answered by psychiatry, the problem of cause is answered by existentialism and the mystery of religion is explained away by secularism.

With the absence of mystery, man has to look elsewhere for his questions about his own being. "Who am I?" is answered by, "You are the person that you are continually becoming." Man is no longer told he is a sinner. The problem of the conscience becomes the problem of consciousness. The problems of the church are no longer spiritual in nature but are answered through sociological research.

As liberal theologians continued to place the mystery of God outside their consideration, more and more Americans vacated their sanctuaries. Some Americans drifted into a pleasure life, while other Americans sought answers outside the church, such as the Jesus Freaks, Campus Crusade, Youth for Christ, fellowship groups, charismatic meetings and other varieties of interdenominational activities.

When secularism first made its impact, denominational churches continued in their traditional religious symbols, but now that worship services are becoming more secular, people are looking elsewhere for the answers previously found in the mystery of Christianity.

Is the Hour Too Late?

Perhaps it is too late to stop the influence of secularism in the American society; maybe the mainline denominations have passed the point of no return and a mercy-killing is justified. If so, the only hope in the future is the raising up of new super-aggressive churches that have returned to the original mystery of Christianity. These churches can answer man's dilemma through the supernatural. The basic assumption of these churches is that God has revealed Himself. Man's salvation is found in God's forgiveness of sin.

But suppose secularism begins to invade the new super-fast-growing churches that are being established. Is the process an endless cycle, with new churches being established when the old churches slip into deterioration? If so, then the only deterrent to the cycle is to understand the processes by which secularization originally came into our churches.

What are the "carriers" of a secularized religion? Some mistakenly see the vehicle of secularization as the Puritan ethic or Protestant value (the terms are synonymous). Those who criticize the Puritan ethic claim the Bible is the source of the success-orientation found in Americans and that man's ultimate satisfaction is achievement, thus leading to secularization. Those who criticize this position do not feel that the Puritan ethic is a reflection of the biblical ethic.

The second "carrier" of secularization is the industrial society in which we live. As America has expanded its capitalistic-industrial economy, the workman looks more and more to his employer for his needs in life. He is less and less dependent upon God. The industrial economy is bent on production and consumer buying. The life-style of America leads to a vicious cycle of stimulating the customer to buy new products, so the industrial complex can continue making a profit, hence producing more goods to be coaxed on the American public. When the morality of Christianity is left out of the picture, society becomes more secular. Eternal values are no longer the dominant force behind society, so a new ethic is needed to justify the emerging life-style. Since a life devoted to consumerism is opposed to the life of the New Testament, the industrial complex dictates the content of America's life-style. The workman's desire is conditioned by past patterns, and he continues to buy to gain pleasure, spiralling the economy into secularism.

The Public School System

A third "carrier" for secularism's growth is the public school system in America. Prior to this century, the church was one of the major sources of education of the masses. One of the reasons for the rapid growth of the Sunday School was that untold multitudes of people learned to read by attending Sunday School, where they read the Word of God. Church education had inclusive goals. The public school was not as competitive as the church. The public school was cooperative in nature with all of the forces of society. The church had been self-centered and sectarian, but the public school was community-centered. Just as the church was established to build a community life out of religious beliefs, now the public school set up a religious belief out of the community life. (However, this was the religion of secularism.) The public school effectively used all of the forces and facilities at its command, including the church, and became the leveling force for the American way of life.

In the early days, the public schools made use of the mystery of Christianity, and when she gained strength, the mystery was repudiated, leaving God out of the picture.

The public school and supernaturalism are polarized against each other. The foundation of secular education is truth found by the pragmatic process; the basis of Christianity is the revelation found in the Word of God. Whereas the public school must adapt itself to the needs of all children, the church ministers to all but demands that they adapt to its standards. Public education centers on this life, while the church prepares a man for the next world. In recent years the public school has been militantly rejecting any influence of the church: i.e., Bible reading, prayers,

Christmas programs, etc. In the future the church will have to fight back, rejecting the suffocating influence of secularism.

Today, those denominational churches that continue to follow the inclusive policies of the public school system will be eaten up by its secularism, while those churches which resist "Deweyism" can grow and find expansion in the days to come.

The American school system is unique and for the first time in the history of education, a system of public instruction has been created which rigidly excludes the religion of the people. By a very devious system of first incorporation and finally exclusion, religion has been put out of the public school system.

Public school education decries sectarianism in any form and claims to represent democracy, all of the people. That is, all of the people except the religious ones. The religion of secularism is diametrically opposed to sectarianism and works to project a common denominator outside of Christ. Sectarianism is defined as undue denominationalism, which is defined as having an extravagant view of one's own religion, bigotry, intolerance, or fanaticism.

Conclusion

The church does not depend upon the outside world for its existence or growth. The church depends upon its relationship to Christ who claimed, "All power is given unto me in heaven and in earth" (Matt. 28:18). Thus, the church becomes a dynamic force. Men look to Jesus Christ for power to bring the church into existence and then transforming the world in which the church lives. The Puritan ethic, upon which the American society was founded, was a result of the formidable processes of the Christian church. The Pilgrims, along with other founding fathers, came for religious liberty, an open Bible in their hands and a consciousness of God in their hearts. Harvard, the first institution of higher learning, was established so that young men might be prepared for the ministry, to carry on the church after those trained in England had passed off the scene. The church helped create the American society in which it existed. During the last 20 years we have seen a reversal in this procedure. The church that was a force in forming society is now dependent upon it. Christian principles helped found our nation, but now the formation of our society is being controlled by secularism. Some liberal theologians now advocate secular social action to renew America apart from traditional church influence. Even though the liberal minister claims to be following the role of New Testament prophets, the basis of their sermons are found in pragmatic secularism rather than New Testament Christianity.

We can only expect secularism to produce a man-centered religion. Mystery is denied. The extreme results of secularism are black militant preachers, occultism, lawless demonstrations in the name of the church, and exhibitionism during worship services. Secularism controls mainline denominations and is the cause for decreased attendance, membership and offerings.

NOTES

1. Charles Morrison, *The Unfinished Reformation* (New York: Harper and Brothers, Publisher, 1953), p. 36.

2. Peter L. Berger, *The Sacred Canopy* (Garden City, New York: Doubleday & Company, Inc., 1969), p. 128.

3. Paul Tillich, *Systematic Theology,* vols. 1–3 (Chicago: University of Chicago Press, 1951–63).

4. John Robinson, *Honest to God* (London: SCM Press, 1963).

5. Harvey Cox, *The Secular City* (New York: Macmillan, 1965).

6. Charles Y. Glock, *To Comfort and to Challenge* (Berkeley: University of California Press, 1967).

CHAPTER 7

The Growth of Bureaucracy

(The Sociological Cycle of Church Growth)

Parable of the Life-Saving Station

On a dangerous seacoast where shipwrecks often occur there was once a crude little lifesaving station. The building was just a hut, and there was only one boat, but the few devoted members kept a constant watch over the sea, and with no thought for themselves they went out day or night tirelessly searching for the lost. Many lives were saved by this wonderful little station, so that it became famous. Some of those who were saved, and various others in the surrounding area, wanted to associate and give their time and money. New boats were brought and new crews were trained. The little lifesaving station grew.

Some of the new members of the lifesaving station were unhappy that the building was so crude and so poorly equipped. They felt that a more comfortable place should be provided as the first refuge of those saved from the sea. So they replaced the emergency cots with beds and put better furniture in an enlarged building. Now the lifesaving station became a popular gathering place for its members, and they redecorated it beautifully and furnished it exquisitely. Fewer members were now interested in going on lifesaving missions, so they hired lifeboat crews. The lifesaving motif still prevailed in the club decoration and there was a liturgical lifesaving boat in the meeting room. About this time, a large ship was wrecked off the coast, and the hired crews brought in boatloads of cold, wet and half-drowned people. They were dirty and sick and some of them had yellow skin. The beautiful new club was considerably messed up. So the

95

property committee immediately had a shower house built outside the club where victims of shipwreck could be cleaned up before coming inside.

At the next meeting, there was a split in the club membership. Most of the members wanted to stop the club's lifesaving activities as being unpleasant and a hindrance to the normal social life of the club. Some members insisted upon lifesaving as their primary purpose and pointed out that they were still called a lifesaving station. But they were finally voted down and told that if they wanted to save lives of all the various kinds of people who were shipwrecked in those waters, they could begin their own lifesaving station down the coast. They did.

As the years went by, the new station experienced the same changes that had occurred in the old. It evolved into a club, and yet another lifesaving station was founded. History continued to repeat itself, and today you will find a number of exclusive clubs along that shore. Shipwrecks are still frequent in those waters, but most of the people drown!

Rev. T. O. Wedel, Warden, College of Preachers
Washington Cathedral, Washington, D.C.

Parable of Church Growth

On a dangerous dark side street near the steel mill located between two taverns was a crude little storefront church building. Wooden folding chairs were set up, a crude pulpit constructed, and a few devoted members prayed constantly for the salvation of transient millworkers. With no thought for self or pleasure, the members went out visiting continually in every home, speaking to reach lost people for Jesus Christ. Many were converted and when a notorious gambler was converted, the little mission became famous. Christians from surrounding areas commuted to the church, giving their time, money, and effort. New pews were bought and ushers were trained. The little mission purchased the shop next door and doubled its auditorium size.

Some of the new members were unhappy with the crude building and poor equipment. It was said in a congregational meeting, "A man can better worship God in a comfortable pew in an air-conditioned auditorium." Matching chancel furniture was donated when new pews were installed. The members redecorated with tinted glass windows, adding Christian education facilities and a parking lot. The members lost interest in visitation, so they hired young zealous preachers to do their work. A revival was held and a man of God preached repentance. Perspiring mill hands were led to the Lord and when high school greasers started attending regularly, the deacons complained, not wanting their daughters to be contaminated. Small kids brought by Sunday School buses did not have shoes or clean clothes. The Women's Missionary Union immediately installed a "millworkers' closet" so the needy could put on proper clothes. But the women were critical when the immaculately clean floors were muddied.

At the next congregational meeting some members wanted the pastor to quit evangelistic preaching, wanting a more dignified, reverent worship service. Other members insisted soul winning was the primary purpose of the church. They were finally voted down and told to go elsewhere. "After all, millworkers like sensationalism," remarked a bank vice-president. They rented a store building across the street and began services with only crude folding chairs and a small pulpit. As the years went by the new mission experienced the same changes that had occurred in the old. It evolved into a religious club and yet another soul winning station was founded. History continued to repeat itself, and if you visit the mill section today you will find a number of exclusive sophisticated churches. Because of the neighborhood, none of those who attend the exclusive churches live there, but have moved to the better parts of the town. It was determined that not one of the millworkers in the neighborhood attends a single church in the area.

The parable of the life-saving station has an amazing parallel with the Christian church. A dynamic purpose of saving life slowly erodes into a social club. Dedicated workmen brave the elements to seek drowning, helpless victims. The unfolding drama of men against the sea changes over a period of time. The men no longer go to the sea in ships. The act of rescue is pantomimed on a stage before audiences; the boatmen are play-actors; the lost victims only repeat lines to convince the hearers of their sincerity. Thus, saving the lost becomes an empty ritual surrounded with symbols and meaningless pledges. Many mainline denominational churches simply play-act salvation; few people are ever converted.

The thesis of this volume is that churches deteriorate for several reasons: growing secularism, a departure from original purposes, the changing purpose of churches, the changing role of pastors, the changing nature of American society and the socialization process whereby individuals of strong conscience become a religious institution. This last factor, the sociological cycle of church growth, is considered in this chapter.

Observers note that churches go through a process of socialization whereby groups that begin with a high fervency of religious devotion evolve through a process of time into an institutional church. The church founded upon warm fervor to God ends up as a cold humanitarian organization; that which was begun on revivalistic principles ends up as a rational social club. Ernst Troeltsch, the German philosopher-sociologist, was one of the first observers to translate this deterioration into a principle.[2] He maintained that churches began as a sect and evolved into *ecclesia* or a denominational stage.

The Cycle Pattern

There is an inner strength found in churches at the beginning of the sociological cycle where members' strong dedication to God is reflected in sacrificial service to the church. These churches grow in attendance, offering and membership. Troeltsch called these *sectarian churches*. With the passing of time, the sectarian church moves to the second stage on the cycle, called the *institutional church*, the congregation still retains the doctrinal distinctives of the sect, along with much of its vitality; however, Christianity becomes more rational. The institutional church becomes organized and structured. The original purpose of the church is retained, but an efficient administration keeps the church in motion. The third stage of the cycle is called by Troeltsch the *denomination* stage, representing a group of churches banded together to accomplish corporately what can't be accomplished by individual congregations. Troeltsch and other sociologists have painted a negative image of denominationalism. Even though there are pure motives for forming a denomination, churches usually allow a gradual centralization of control and direction. Decision-making authority slips from the founding members to the professional clergymen at headquarters, who give more attention to the form of Christianity than to its function. The final stage in the cycle is called *deterioration*. Institutional blight settles through the social structure of the movement. Institutional blight is the process of social decay where individuals, committees and churches lose sight of the original goals of the founding fathers. The denomination becomes senile and deterioration sets in.

When the denomination is unable to find a *reason for existence*, the whole superstructure drifts and there is no internal strength to hold it together or to give it new direction. Voices within the denomination cry for a return to the original precepts, yet these prophets appear to have a hollow cry because no one will heed them. One has observed that such denominations have an *identity crisis*. People lose interest because their spiritual needs are not satisfied; attendance drops and with it the resulting decline in offerings. After attendance goes down, then membership declines and next there are economy moves to cut back programs and close down missions and churches that cannot meet the budget. New candidates for the ministry are difficult to find and churches go without pastors. Then the high standards for the ministry are sacrificed in order to get somebody to "fill the pulpit." Moberg, the church sociologist at Marquette University, describes the process of deterioration as: "diseases which show symptoms of the stage are: formalism, indifference, obsolescence, absolutism, red tape, patronage and corruption."[3] The denominations die peaceably, members drift away, no new converts take their place. Children drop out of Sunday School, and when the parents pass away the pews are empty. The denomination, like the senior citizen who dies in Florida, is unknown and lonely; few attend the funeral.

On the other hand, some denominations feel paralysis setting in. The younger generation, unable to identify with the principles that originally formed the catalyst, search for a new reason for existence. These young turks bring on an ecclesiastical rebellion. They throw over the old religion and embrace the new. Radical theology brings in a social-oriented ministry. Yet their ministry alienates the remaining members, who in turn cut off finances and in a final desperation drop out of attendance.[4]

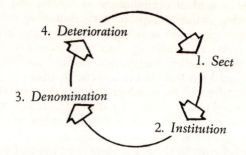

At the first stage of the cycle are found sectarian churches which are similar to modern-day fundamentalism. These churches have the ability for dynamic numerical growth, both in founding new churches and producing growth in existing congregations. Although not all fundamental churches are growing, the seeds of growth are found at this stage of the cycle.

The institutional church found at the second stage of the cycle has the capacity for growth; however, it is not usually growing as fast as fundamentalism. Also, not all evangelical churches are growing. Most evangelical denominations are "holding their own," while a few are pushing the growth chart upward. Many of the new denominations of the National Association of Evangelicals, Wheaton, Illinois, are institutional in nature. This position has been called neo-evangelical, a term of repute by fundamentalists; however, no evangelical calls himself a neo-evangelical.

The Denominational Stage

Denominationalism is the third step on the cycle, usually representing liberalism or mainline denominations in the United States. At the beginning of this stage there is some dynamic and as a result continued numerical growth because of organizational efficiency; however, toward the end of the cycle the growth indicator points downward. Churches in the denominational stage do not have the spiritual dynamics to attract individuals. These churches have lost their mystery. The erosion of secularism has taken its toll. Whatever growth a denominational church experiences is usually because of external reasons in the organization rather than internal motivation because individuals are having their spiritual needs met. David Moberg, has described the cycle as "the process by which cults originate, develop into sects, and then change into denominations, finally perhaps to emerge from the process as churches." [5]

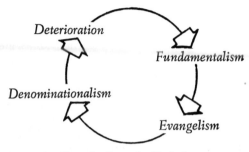

Deterioration

Fundamentalism

Denominationalism

Evangelism

Church Growth Cycle [6]

Why Sects Grow

The word sect means "a narrow religious group" or "a church dissenting from the established church or society in general." At the very heart and core of sectarian churches is rebellion against the accepted way of life and repudiation of the established church. Sectarians' beliefs are different . . . their life-style is different . . . their values are different . . . and their destination is different. A sectarian Christian gives allegiance to God who lives in heaven. The mystery of Christianity is inherent in his existence. Out of a "hard-headed commitment" a sectarian Christian does not mind being different from the crowd; as a matter of fact, his Christianity calls for him to separate himself because he believes the godly life is distinctive.

The sectarian church is in opposition to the established church because of its hypocrisy and deadness. They feel the religion of the establishment attacked the Lord and crucified Christ. The religious persecution of the early church by the Jews is seen as similar to the attacks by the established church on fundamentalist groups. The scribes and Pharisees are likened unto liberal preachers.

Sectarian church doctrine demands that individuals separate themselves from what is called the evil world system.[7] The fundamentalist believes that sin is the root problem for man's present dilemma. Sin does more than send a man to hell; sin is the cause for all individual social injustices. Corporate injustices are also the result of man's corporate sin and when men lie, steal, rape or cheat on their income tax, it is the expression of man's unthwarted sinful nature. The duty of the sectarian church is to preach personal regeneration and when individuals are personally transformed, they become the leaven that uplifts all of human society. But when sin is allowed to grow unhindered, it destroys the individual, it destroys the family and will ultimately destroy the church and nation. Therefore, the sectarian Christian believes he must separate himself from any form of iniquity and transgression. The apex of iniquity is found in breaking the Ten Commandments. Even though the fundamentalist appears legalistic, he must not allow the influence of sin to pollute his life. "Abstain from all appearance of evil" (I Thess. 5:22).

Sin Will Run Its Course

The sectarian Christian believes that sin will ultimately run its course, the world going through a time of severe tribulation when God's wrath shall judge sin; then Christ shall return bodily to earth to redeem Christians and judge all unbelievers, sending them to the lake of fire which burns forever. One can never understand a fundamentalist without perception into what motivates him. Since he feels sin is the cause of man's problem, he is motivated to seek its solution.

Because of their separation from society, fundamentalists are seldom understood and at times attacked. The sect is usually persecuted because of its fierce religious devotion and unique beliefs. Frequently, persecution reinforces their separatist stand. Their feeling that the world is ungodly reinforces their semi-ascetic attitude towards the world. As a result the sect prefers isolation from the world rather than compromise with it.

The sectarian is theologically unprogressive, inasmuch as his authority is found in a historic revelation which is incapsulated in the pages of Scripture. As a result fundamentalists care little for the latest theological discourses. They do not look to sociological research to give them information regarding church growth. Sectarians follow the rules of Scripture to build a church. Dallas Billington, a layman with eighth-grade education, built the world's largest Sunday School by applying Acts 5:42, "And daily in the temple, and in every house, they ceased not to teach and preach Jesus Christ." He simply visited every home in Akron, Ohio, and led people to Jesus Christ. Those of the sects are committed biblicists, holding the verbal, plenary inspiration of Scripture as the ultimate basis for truth. Religious leaders who reject this authority are excluded from their fellowship. As a result sectarian Christians may appear to be unprogressive or anti-intellectual in their Christianity. They see the educational community, including universities and theological seminaries, as enemies of the Word of God, thus making the fundamentalists enemies of education. Whereas some fundamentalists carry on a running battle with local educational institutions, the fight is not so much with the educators, it is with the threat that the fundamentalists see to their position.

Fundamentalist churches are based on personal loyalty by every member, to the exclusion of all alternatives. Members are not to place P.T.A. or recreation above the church. The minister does not care whether his people are loyal out of proper reasons, such as a knowledge of doctrine, or for improper reasons—guilt, ignorance or false teaching—just so long as the member is loyal.

Loyalty is usually expressed in enthusiasm and/or wholehearted obedience. As a result, fundamentalist churches are experience-centered in their service. In the revivalistic services shouts of "Amen" are heard and hand-waving is seen. The speakers use jokes and humor to motivate the congregation. "A man ought to enjoy his religion," states John Rawlings of Landmark Baptist Temple, Cincinnati. Zeal is the criterion for spiritual service. Much time is spent on making announcements to motivate Christians to attend every service or reach lost people for the Lord.

Salvation Is an Experience

Fundamentalists define salvation as "a conversion experience which prepares a man for heaven." A man must be "saved" to become a fundamentalist; he does not join the church as one joins a denominational church. To become a member of a sectarian church, a man must be "born again" (John 3:1–7), which requires an involvement of the entire personality: intellect, emotions and will. Whereas denominations emphasize intellectual Christianity, the fundamentalists maintain that more than knowledge is needed for salvation. *Knowledge of God* is the first step in salvation; a man must know the plan of salvation, including the sacrificial death of Christ, His bodily burial and supernatural resurrection. *Emotion* is the second step, whether the response be love, crying, joy, or remorse for sins. A man's total being is affected; as a result he may hate sin or love God—both are emotions. The final step in salvation is a commitment of the *will;* some ministers preach, "A man must be broken." Others maintain, "You must be yielded." Whatever the terminology, man's will must be in subjection to God. His will must respond to God and he "must receive Jesus Christ" (John 1:12).

One indication that a church is slipping from the sect stage into denominationalism is when "mental belief" or agreement with the doctrinal statement is substituted for a conversion experience. Members of a sect join because of personal regeneration and identification with a new moral ethic.

Max Weber observed this in his one visit to America in 1904. He noted that in all types of relationships, whether business, social or religious, most people usually raise the question, "Where do you attend church?" He also concluded that American sect membership was a guarantee of personal moral qualities, especially those qualities required for success in business. He noted that credit was more readily advanced to sect members than others, and that those who were expelled from the sect usually suffered economic and social loss in the community. Of course, such standing is not true today.

Since the sectarian feels man must have an emotional conversion, some fundamentalist ministers resort to sensationalism in the pulpit, to move the hearts of hearers. Also, fundamentalists have been accused of using "bawdy church music" rather than liturgy, ritualism and anthems. Fundamentalism has developed a "religious folk-style" all its own, aimed at moving the heart and speaking to man's nature, rather than the classical religious music with robed choirs, threefold Amens and the use of Bach, Beethoven and Mozart. Moberg describes the church-community of the fundamentalist/sectarian.

> Each sect is a moral community which is suspicious of rival sects and ready to exclude unworthy members. Sects have unspecialized, nonprofessional, part-time ministers. Emphasizing evangelism, conversion, and voluntary confessional joining, their chief concern is with an "adult" membership. They adhere to such strict biblical standards as tithing or nonresistance . . . congregational participation in church administration and services is at a high level. Fervor, reliance upon spontaneous guidance of the Holy Spirit, and use of contemporary folk music are characteristic of their religious services. They emphasize religion in the home and also have a comparatively large number of special religious services, so the sect assumes hegemony over large spheres of its members' time.[8]

In Gaston County, North Carolina, Pope wrote in his book *Millhands and Preachers* that a number of Protestant denominations and sects were moving toward the denominational type, away from sectarian characteristics at varying degrees of change. These involved Free Will Baptists, Pentecostal Holiness, Church of God, Independent Tabernacles, Wesleyan Methodists, and Baptists. He noted that Baptists had changed more than any other denomination in the country.

Pope noted that with increasing sectarianism he found increased monthly church attendance, decreased membership in organizations outside the church, choice of five closest friends from the membership of the same church, and more satisfaction from the church than any other type of social participation.[9]

The Question of the Poor

Because fundamentalism is based on emotionalism and blind loyalty, the outside observer notes that their clientele are basically the poor or ignorant. Those who criticize them will equate naivete and/or ignorance with fundamentalism, hence discounting the validity of sectarianism. Many present-day denominational churches were one time equated with the lower class. But the transforming experience of salvation makes the lower-class Christian a candidate for upward social mobility. His piety of life and a close identification with the church gives the fundamentalist stability in the community. His ignorance is eradicated by his new church life-style. Indoctrination and pulpit stimulation give him new knowledge. He is usually dedicated to the new biblical knowledge and becomes intolerant of any other position, hence supporting his loyalty to the church. The result of biblical knowledge is social stability, making him a prospect for the middle class. He settles down in his job, buys a house, becomes concerned about his kids' education, and eliminates his boozing and revelry.

But even if sectarian churches are made up of the poor, this does not make them second-class religious institutions. Jesus spent much of His time with the poor. He indicated the rich man had as much difficulty entering into heaven as the camel passing through the eye of a needle (Mark 10:25). There are a number of Scriptures that criticize the rich (Matt. 13:22; James 5:1–4) and commend the poor (James 2:1–4).

Also, the poor are more aware of the harshness of life: lack of food, adequate shelter, financial security and the good times that money can bring. Money may bring a false sense of security to the affluent whereby he isolates himself from the ultimate questions and the issues of eternity. The rich can live in a plastic world, created by their wealth, leading to self-sufficiency and spiritual independence. As a result, the rich do not feel the need for God as do the poor; therefore, the fundamentalist church that speaks of the mysteries of God and offers transformation to the individual will attract the poor.

Born Among the Masses

Sociology teaches us that sectarian movements are usually born among the masses found at the lower spectrum of the socioeconomic continuum. When the poor find their stability in Jesus Christ, they move upward in social mobility. Their churches become more affluent and, over several generations and through the process of time, whole denominations, such as the Methodist church, move up the socio-economic ladder. At one time Methodists were known as the poor and alienated in England and among the American frontier people. Today the Methodists are associated with the upper-middle-class of society. Since money may give a false sense of security to the affluent, the denomination built on rich suburbanites no longer needs the security that was previously found in God.

The strength of sects is their warm revivalistic meetings and their weakness is usually superficial education. The sect/fundamentalist churches have a reputation for inferior education but numerical growth, as noted Clark.

> Although their religious education is a very poor quality in terms of philosophy, curriculum materials, and teaching methods, many sects survive and flourish, often out-stripping in rate of growth the denominations that adhere to the very latest organizations and principles of religious education.[10]

In an earlier book *The Ten Largest Sunday Schools*,[11] the author noted that the largest Sunday Schools in America were sectarian in nature and in a later book, *America's Fastest Growing Churches*,[12] the author showed that the fastest growing churches were also sectarian. These churches not only are growing but have better-than-average educational programs; this is the reason for their growth and large size. However, the danger of fundamentalist/sectarians is their emotional-based Christianity. They have an emotional commitment to Christianity and as long as their dedication is in keeping with Scripture, God can bless them. However, some fundamentalist/sectarian ministers go off on tangents (i.e., Sunday School gimmicks, doctrinal deviations, theological witch-hunting, etc.), and their commitment is no longer to the Word of God, even though they are still sincere and surrendered to the Lord. Their lack of doctrinal understanding will put them on the shelf, as far as the blessing of God. The fundamentalist needs to progress to the rational Christianity of the evangelical without damaging his spirit he has received from the fundamentalists.

The Institutional/Evangelical

The second step on the sociological cycle is *institutional-evangelical,* generally applied to Christians, including some fundamentalists, whose doctrinal distinctives fall within the historic framework of Christianity, but whose methodology has changed. The institutional Christian includes evangelicals, conservatives, orthodox and neo-evangelicals. These have made their peace with the world and have become established in the communities. Even though evangelicals might have more tolerance for the outside world and other religious bodies, they are still known for their "old-fashioned beliefs." The sectarian Christian is similar in doctrine to the institutional Christian; their differences come in religious practice or life-style. Even though the institutional Christian gives allegiance to supernatural Christianity, he has lost some of the mystery in its daily outworking.

At the turn of the century, liberalism was a system of theological belief that permeated the seminaries and had captured many of the sophisticated churches within mainline denominations. With the growth of secularism in America (see chapter "The Loss of Mystery), liberalism captured more and more local churches. To meet this rising tide of anti-biblical belief, a group of men began fellowshipping around an apologetic defense of historical Christianity. Most of these defenders of the faith were found in mainline denominational churches, even though some of them were found in independent churches. Men such as William B. Riley, William Biederwolf, Arno C. Gaebelein, William Pettingill, and J. Frank Norris began a passionate plea for churches to return to the orthodox fundamentals of the faith. Their main platform was *The Fundamentals,* a magazine which became the rallying point for theological conservatives. In addition to the magazine, some men made their doctrine known through radio programs, revival meetings, Bible conferences and Bible conference grounds such as Winona Lake Conference. Out of the title *The Fundamentals* came the name "fundamentalist" that referred to a conservative enlightened position concerning historic orthodox Christianity. Over a period of time, the term *fundamentalist* grew into a negative connotation.

Carl F. H. Henry, past editor of *Christianity Today* became a severe critic of fundamentalism and identified it with not only theology, but a negative life-style, by stating, "Historically fundamentalism was a theological position; only gradually did the movement come to signify a mood and disposition as well." [13] Later Henry described fundamentalism both theologically and methodologically:

Fundamentalism is considered a summary term for theological pugnaciousness, ecumenic disruptiveness, also unprogressiveness, scientific obliviousness, and/or anti-intellectual inexcusableness. By others, fundamentalism is equated with extreme dispensationalism, pulpit sensationalism, accepted emotionalism, social withdrawal, and bawdy church music. [14]

The term *fundamentalist* became a slur against an individual; however, those who were fundamentalists were proud of the label.

The theological world divided itself into liberals and fundamentalists, those to the right and those to the left section of the theological spectrum. Theological in-fighting existed over the issue of seven literal days' creation, the literal inspiration of Scripture, the vicarious substitutionary atonement, the virgin birth of Jesus Christ, the bodily resurrection and the bodily premillennial return of Jesus Christ. For 50 years from the turn of the century till the mid-fifties, the two camps polarized themselves and individuals found themselves on one side of the theological fence or the other. However, during the 1950's a new camp of theologians grew up, attempting an ecclectic position, taking the theology of the fundamentalists and secular-humanism found in liberalism. This mid-camp, called "evangelicals," also was called "neo-evangelical" by its enemies; however, an evangelical never calls himself a neo-evangelical.

The Fundamentalist Revival

Arnold Hearn, writing in the *Christian Century*, 1948, indicates that there was a "fundamentalist renaissance" which he indicated was a "revival" (his term) going on among theologians on the right. This revival concerned scholarship and scientific investigation of the serious problems surrounding Scripture.[15] Hearn was recognizing the new movements among fundamentalism, even though he was unaware of the growing group of evangelicals.

William Hordern, professor of systematic theology, Garrett Theological Seminary, Evanston, Illinois, wrote in *New Directions for Theology Today*, that there was a new phase of conservatism. He claimed as far back as 1966 that fundamentalism was growing. He saw growing church attendance, higher per capita giving among fundamentalists and a number of young ministerial candidates as a sign of fundamentalist revival. Hordern said,

> Fundamentalism was pronounced dead, and it was assumed that it would soon disappear from the sanctuaries in the hinterlands. To those who were writing the obituaries of fundamentalism, there were disturbing signs.[16]

Hordern lived in the Greater Chicago area and observed the change in conservative churches in Chicago. Whereas Chicago had been the home of fundamentalism, the movement began to change its posture. Some fundamentalists went to Garrett Theological Seminary to study for the ministry, these young men were not anti-intellectual as many prior fundamentalists. Also, the movement left extreme dispensationalism, pulpit sensationalism, softened its lines on separation. Hordern characterized these changes:

> During the fifties, however, a group of young scholars arose from the fundamentalist circles to forge a new theology. These scholars rejected the term "fundamentalist" because they felt that it had become a term of abuse and not a meaningful description of a theological position. Furthermore, they were conscious of the shortcomings of their theological fathers and wished to remold the tradition. They were as concerned as the liberals of an earlier day were to make Christianity relevant to the modern age, but they were determined not to repeat what they saw as the errors of liberalism. Although most of these young men came from fundamentalist seminaries and colleges, they began taking

graduate degrees at nonfundamentalist institutions. They returned to their denominations and seminaries to revitalize the theology that had hardened during the fundamentalist-modernist controversy. There is no agreed name . . . They prefer the name "evangelical" or "new evangelical." [17]

Spiritual Riches to Rags

The institutional Christian is usually a second-generation Christian born into the family of first-generation sect members. His parents were saved from raw heathenism and they became members of a narrow-practicing church. The parents were disillusioned with the deceptive allurement of secularism. They repudiated the old and embraced the new. They didn't need a course in apologetics to prove the existence of God; He lived in their hearts. Their children, born into the church, and for the most part born again, never had the opportunity to experience the "pleasures of sin for a season."

As children they were taught righteousness; therefore the children did not have an emotional conversion experience. Time causes fundamental churches to become evangelical. Second-generation families hold their convictions less deeply. Children born into these families take a different posture; they must be educated, whereas previously others came into the sect by conversion. There is a deep desire on the part of families that their children "obey" the teaching of the church; therefore, the sect takes on a disciplinary organization. The new generation must conform to the ideas and customs of the old. Usually, the children follow in the footsteps of their parents; however, they hold convictions less fervently than the pioneers of the sect, whose beliefs were formulated in the heat of conflict. But children want to be like other children outside the church and with each succeeding generation, it becomes more difficult for the sect to isolate themselves from the world. Training children to become good sect members becomes a problem. The fervency of the movement disappears by the second or third generation. The early rigid entrance requirements usually give way to compromise. In the old days they lowered the age of "adult baptism" among the Baptists. Among other groups, standards regarding worldliness are no longer demanded and, among the Presbyterians, communicant classes are no longer required. By the time the process is completed, the sect has become a denomination.

Survival of the Institution

Perpetuation becomes a dominant motivation in the institutional church. As a sect, they sacrifice and slave to build their church. People give their time to actually construct buildings by the sweat of their brow. Hours are spent in study of the Scriptures and fellowship with like-faith sect members. No sacrifice is too great for the furtherance of the church. Over a period of time, the sect members see their vision evolve into reality. The building goes up, the congregation and the church gain respectability. As the members grow older, they want the church to remain true to its original beliefs; they turn their thoughts to perpetuation. New leaders must be trained to take the place of the old. Their ideals must be translated into words, hence they write out the documents that are found in an institution: first, the history; second, a doctrinal statement; third, operational features; and fourth, standards of behavior. In the early days of the sect, members could identify sin and how to abstain from all appearances of evil. When the church grew, new members had difficulty understanding the reasons for separation from the world, hence standards and rules are written to guide individual behavior.

What have we seen? The sect that was born as a protest against candles, choir robes, and stained glass windows soon has its own ritual. The informal religious services become repetitive patterns; the same people pray, the same type of songs are sung and the customary pattern of the morning service becomes an anti-ritualistic formalism. It may be called the "order of worship" but its ritual is just as perpetual as the ceremonialism of the high church and its written prayers. These religious practices give security and strength to its worshippers. They find meaning and self-expression through their weekly pattern. However, their children and grandchildren hold to its meanings less tenaciously, and after a while the new ritualism has become as meaningless as the old ritualism.

Desire for Stability

Desire for stability is a third factor that pushes a church into the institutional orbit. Whereas the fundamentalist sect was emotional, now sophistication sets in. The members desire community recognition. They no longer want to be known as "wild-eyed" Baptists. The evangelical church attempts to polish up its image and lose its reputation of being militant. "We don't want to be known as fanatics," stated a pastor in Chicago. His church had once been known for street preaching but his members became sophisticated property owners, and respectability became the order of the day.

The evangelical is concerned about interpersonal relationships. In the old sect, the members were concerned about obedience to the Word of God. The primary purpose of the fundamentalist church was the believer's duty to God, expressed through service to the church. His relationship with other sect members was functional, to accomplish the goals of the church. The personhood of others was coincidental, even though it was meaningful. With the passing of time, the Christian realizes the measure of a man's life is found in deep relationships with other men. The institutional Christian begins to move into a new, refreshing world; he realizes that the individual is of supreme worth, both others and himself. A sense of meaning in life is found through dialogue, defined by Reuel Howe, "the meeting of meaning," where two individuals come to know and accept one another for their meaning of life.

A New Area of Tolerance

Growing out of interpersonal relationships is a new area of tolerance. The fundamentalist sect is known for its dogged allegiance to orthodoxy. The evangelical realizes that others can be born-again Christians and disagree in some fringe areas. The narrow-minded Baptist talks to a Pentecostal and finds that they both want to win souls, even though the Pentecostal believes in the baptism of the Holy Spirit and speaking in tongues. The fundamental Baptist realizes that if he is to have fellowship with the Pentecostal, he should not be so narrow in his fellowship. The fundamentalist becomes an evangel. Thus the circle of acceptance grows; those who have deviant attitudes towards eschatology or dispensationalism are accepted by the evangelical. They accept the fact—much to their shock—that a man could be saved, yet not believe in the complete inerrancy of Scripture or he could be a Christian and have a willingness to re-examine the scientific hypothesis of the Scriptures. Whereas the fundamentalist might attack his new friends for "pussyfootin' around with liberalism" the neo-evangelical accepts a broader tolerance and cooperative action with those who do not agree exactly with him. Moberg notes the metamorphosis a sect makes on its way to deterioration.

> The sect originates in social unrest and modulates itself to rival organizations; when it is tolerated and tolerant, it assumes the form of a denomination.[18]

The evangelical/institutional Christian is motivated by rational appeals to the intellect. The fundamentalist is often motivated by his feelings. He is converted under *hard* preaching because he *feels* an uneasiness about sin. When the fundamentalist Christian has an emotional conversion, feelings become a high authority in his life. However, the institutional Christian is usually second generation. He grows up in the Christian home, attending Sunday School and church. These children have never experienced outward sin: i.e. drinking, swearing, sexual deviation or other named sins. They make decisions for Jesus Christ at their mother's knee or in the Sunday School class. They understand the story of salvation and respond accordingly. Their salvation is usually rationally based, therefore they become more intellectual in their Christian understanding than the fundamentalists. As the children grow older they ask, "Why is smoking a sin?" Across the generation gap, the father is perplexed; he feels deeply (emotionally) that smoking contaminates the temple of God. The father gave it up when he was saved because he felt (emotions) the conviction of sin. Now the son wants an intellectual reason why he should not smoke. The father feels that since Christ has saved him from sin, his son should not want to sin.

However, they have had different experiences, the father speaking from the fundamentalist position, the son reflecting his love for Christ from an evangelical faith.

Gap Between Generations

The daughter comes home from high school and says, "How do you know there is a God?" The mother repeats the words of Billy Graham, "I know God exists because . . . I've talked with Him and He walks with me." This answer from *feelings* frustrates the daughter for she wants a *rational* argument. With time the second generation Christian hammers out his intellectual reasons, becoming a disciple of rationality. The mod youth director speaks to young people, giving reasons why I know I am saved, or reasons why I know the Bible is the Word of God. His rational approach to Christianity meets the needs of young people, whereas the preaching of the older ministers fail to motivate the second-generation kids.

Relevancy is another characteristic of the institutional Christian. With the passing of time, he realizes it is possible to be "heavenly-minded but no earthly good." The father becomes concerned about being out of step with the community, and the mother from the fundamentalist church gets "cabin fever," she wants to get with the girls; separation from sin no longer has meaning to her. There is a world out there that she wants to be a part of. The evangelical comes to the conclusion that Christianity must work in everyday life, it must be relevant. The father asks, "What good is this if I spend every night at the church, yet neglect my son and he goes to hell?"

Corporate Relevancy of the Church

Beyond the personal relevancy comes corporate relevancy—the church must be concerned about meeting the needs of its members. Whereas the fundamentalist feels that the world can be changed by the transformation of the individual, the evangelical points to the Old Testament prophets, indicating that preaching was socially-oriented, aimed at changing society. The church should answer the problems of society. The evangelical Christian finds a biblical mandate for both church social action and a balance with individual concern in the community. He becomes concerned about voter registration, the inner city church, aid for Biafra, and at the same time feels that the church must win souls to Jesus Christ.

One of the dominant characteristics of the institutional church is its organization. Dedication, zeal and involvement hold a religious movement together in its primitive state. The strong charismatic leader solves many church (fundamental) problems; usually he is an efficient leader and organizer. But over a period of time, leaders change and the church assumes a more traditional role in the American society. When the strong pastor leaves or dies, the existing board calls a second pastor, yet does not give him the authority that the founder had. Whereas the first pastor had freedom with the finances, the church elects a finance committee to help the second pastor spend money. As the church grows larger, more paid staff members are needed in area of music, recreation, education, and business management. The paid staff must be integrated with the lay workers. It is not clear whether the specialists are employed because laymen no longer have the zeal to carry out the ministry, or laymen no longer feel needed because there are full-time workers on staff. However, the organization does tend to suffer, even though immediately after hiring professionals, the work seems to go forward. The professional brings his expertise and the work of the church progresses: i.e. he wins souls, gets more in Sunday School or becomes a proficient business manager. Professionals rarely realize they kill the church by their success. As the professional is more efficient, the laymen allow him more freedom, hence the grass-roots control of the church seem to turn brown and begin to die in the ground. Later as the church approaches denominational stature, the laymen lose interest in their church, they stop becoming involved in evangelism, and "institutional blight" affects the church family.

The institutional church has a favorable attitude towards education. They place a high premium upon college education, seminary training, or intellectual attainment. The fundamentalist equates liberalism with academic excellence, and both are sin. He preaches hard against modernism, especially in liberal seminaries and state universities.

Many fundamentalist churches are pastored by men without academic education; two years ago in the listing of the 100 largest Sunday Schools, *Christian Life* Magazine, 1971, 32 pastors from the 100 largest had one year or less of college education. I have maintained that these churches are sectarian in nature; one of their identifying marks is their attitude toward education.

The Need for Knowledge

However, the institutional Christian realizes a liberal arts education is necessary for personal growth; there is a vast world of knowledge that the pastor should know. Fundamentalists tend to go to Bible colleges which give the pastor training in Bible knowledge, theology, Christian education and pastoral duty. Institutional pastors tend to go to Christian liberal arts colleges, where they are broadened: i.e., made men of the world. As churches go into denominations, they build liberal arts colleges and theological seminaries. Over a long involvement of time, rational Christianity replaces emotional Christianity, because the young people from the church are trained in the denominational educational institutions. (One might theorize that the fundamentalists put faith (a term meaning emotional commitment) over reason, whereas the evangelical places reason over blind faith. Those who bow at the shrine of rationality slowly incorporate a higher textual criticism approach to the Scriptures and eventually begin doubting the deity of Christ, the existence of God and the creation of the universe. Because evangelicals are rationally oriented, these issues seem to be their topics of conversation. Fundamentalists fight other battles having to do with "gut-level Christianity;" their concern is more emotional.

Denominational/Liberalism

The third stage on the institutional cycle is called by Troeltsch and Weber *denomination,* symbolizing the growth of centralized government. We have technically defined denomination as:

A denomination is a group of churches with similar doctrinal beliefs, who have similar traditions and backgrounds, who share the same goals in ministry, who desire fellowship to encourage one another, and have organically bound themselves together to establish corporately what they feel cannot be wrought separately.

However, the term in the cycle is broader than the organization of many churches. The term here refers to a stage of development among religious groups who have allowed control to slip from individual churches to a centralized headquarters.

Gouldner notes that there are four processes in institutionalization that bring on a denomination: (1) The organization must grow by imposing formal rules upon its members, producing a conformity among its people that is no longer a product of primarily voluntary action. (2) Bureaucratic growth tends to increase efficiency. (3) A vicious circle of increased formalization may impair the effectiveness that bureaucracy was intended to solve. (4) The institution tends to collapse but goes through renewal efforts to keep itself in existence; along with the renewal comes relaxation of the formal rules.[19]

People join sect churches out of deep spiritual commitment, but the denominational Christian usually joins for secondary reasons.

When a new denomination is being founded, policies, beliefs and aims are usually hammered into statements by men of good will. Pastors feel deeply about religious issues. They meet with other pastors of similar churches and vote to bind their churches together to carry out likeminded purposes. Annual meetings are held for fellowship and determination of policies. Issues are debated on the floor and heated arguments sometimes erupt in committee meetings. Men of good will argue with one another. They seek other delegates to vote for their motion. At the beginning stages the control of the denomination rests in the hands of the pastors and delegates. The denominational official has little voice in policy, if he has not been elected as a delegate from a local church.

Power to the Professional

But, with the passing of time, laymen become willing to allow the professional to carry out duties that originally were controlled by the church. They rationalize, "After all, our officials are experts and have more knowledge in our denomination than average Christians. Why should they not be given liberty to run the show?" Professionals who are given a great amount of liberty should be obligated to the people who gave them their authority. But, again with time, the professional is separated from the opinions of the grass roots. The professional begins to make decisions according to what he feels is best, not according to the people. He becomes more callous to the needs of the individual church member. He feels he has a better understanding of the denomination. The denomination becomes dominated by small groups and the organization becomes similar to a boss-ridden party. Decisions of consequence are made in back-room meetings; the floor of the annual meeting becomes a rubber stamp. If concerned individuals challenge liberalism in the denominational seminary, they are talked down on the floor of the annual meeting. Two years ago the Southern Baptist Convention attempted to change the policies of Broadman Press, the official voice of the Southern Baptist Convention, but to no avail. In a personal interview, Dr. W. A. Criswell told the author that he had felt he could make a conservative impact on the Southern Baptist Convention when he was president of the Convention. However, to his dismay, the bureaucrats in Nashville ran the Convention and he had little say in its basic direction.

Centralization of Authority

The centralization of authority that has occurred in the Federal Government also happens in the denomination. Local communities lose control of their public school districts; their highway programs and welfare responsibilities shift to the Federal Government because Washington has more money, or can set a higher standard of excellency for the good of all people. Following the same argument, the denominational headquarters is said to have a broader perspective of needs, therefore can set a higher standard for all churches. Headquarters can determine the pastor's salary and where finances should be spent. The fallacy of both illustrations is that the Federal Government and the denomination is the sum total of all individuals. The money that Washington gives back is only on taxes that we have paid, and the money spent by the Sunday School secretary is only the tithe that is dropped into hundreds of offering plates throughout the denominations each Sunday morning.

Another place where secularism is creeping into denominations is through its business practice. Internally, denominations function by departments and divisions. Their day-to-day practices are controlled by typical business procedures similar to General Motors or other large corporations. The headquarters building of a denomination appears to look like any other business institution in the city. Rows of secretaries type the endless correspondence with churches and other bureaus. File decks keep records and junior executives supervise the flow of work. The qualities of Jesus Christ supposedly hold many denominations together. Christ was humble, and by his own life-style repudiated wealth, prestige and security. At the sectarian level, pastors are followed by the masses because the preacher not only identifies with Jesus Christ but follows his example. However, at the denominational level, the qualities of Jesus Christ are repudiated; executive secretaries wear the finest clothes, draw salaries that compete with the business world, and the denomination is secure by its portfolio and Dunn and Bradstreet standing.

The public relations office of the denomination creates a good image and the advertising department communicates a polished presentation to all involved. Information offices resist any efforts at being called "lobbying offices," but they do the same duty. Fund-raising officials approach churches, businesses, and foundations. The comptroller is charged with the responsibility of not spending money outside of the budget and the purchasing officer attempts to buy all items as cheaply as possible to save the Lord's treasury.

Similar to the Secular

All the agencies of the denomination are told to "produce." Those who are not successful are not good Christians nor have they been loyal to the trust bestowed by churches. In actuality the denominational office is similar to any other secular organization with its problems and pettiness. Some denominational personnel who begin in their position as service to the Lord, finally view it as a 9:00-to-5:00 job. As a matter of fact, most mainline denominations do not require their employees to belong to one of their churches. Denominations have become "big business" in America, with their portfolio stocks and bonds, their myriad of offices, IBM machines, and latest organizational techniques including flow charts, business forms and mass communication.

In the early days of the denomination, the discipline of its members was used to promote the efficiency of the organization. Now discipline becomes the intrinsic value of the machines. Members were evaluated by their loyalty to their ideals, in the denomination they are evaluated by their loyalty to the institution. As a result, ideals are sometimes submerged to advance the organization. According to Moberg,

> Institutional prosperity becomes the goal, instead of a means to the end of building up people's spiritual life. The bureaucracy is "the tail that wags the dog," keeping the institution in operation even if it has outlived its basic function.[20]

Now we have the denominational headquarters that is similar to a Washington bureau or a New York business. Power has shifted from the Scriptures; it is "the gospel according to Wall Street." Moberg sees this secular-power and observes.

> They (denominations) compromise their ideas by accepting the status quo and establishing themselves alongside the ruling powers of society. Hence most of their influence is not religious but merely secular power in religious garb.[21]

There are die-hard members in every denomination who will, by their very presence, hold back bureaucrats from taking too drastic liberty in their leadership. Even though the "old members" of a denomination have lost their doctrinal distinctives, they rebel at bureaucracy out of bias (action without beliefs) insisting that the denominations fulfill their historic purposes. The control that these traditionalists have over the church is similar to the control that the American purchasing public has over products offered in the supermarket. Denominational officials exercise some self-restraint in light of vocal criticism and traditional pressures.

Differences in Doctrine

The fundamentalist and evangelical usually believe the same doctrinal statement; however, at the denominational level, theology changes. The literal interpretation of Scripture is denied. The Bible is treated as an allegory or a book of symbols. A growing secularism leads to a liberal interpretation of Scripture and the control that doctrine has had over policies is softened. Those who ignore the supernatural are just as damaging to the church as those who have denied the authority of the supernatural.

How does liberal doctrine slip into the church? Subtly. The liberal minister proclaims Christ was raised physically from the grave, although His body remained in the tomb. God created the world by the power of His Word, although an evolutionary process brought the world into existence as we know it today.

The denominational Christian in the pew desires to keep his faith unique, yet be a full citizen of society; he desires to live the Christian life, yet be a full participant in the American way of life. His faith is no longer unique. His life is common among men; he becomes an average American. When the church loses its uniqueness and becomes common, it loses its existence.

The American Mythology

In America, all things are created for the enjoyment of man, and society exists for his advancement and fulfillment. The denominational church reflects the ideology of society, and places man at the center of life. Problems can be analyzed and attacked, arriving at acceptable solutions. After all, if man can orbit the moon and fly faster than the speed of sound, why can he not accomplish any goal to which he diligently applies his resources? The denominational Christian also places high emphasis upon the worth and dignity of man. He gives God token allegiance as Creator and Designer of the universe. But the denominational Christian seldom relies upon the divine for immediate help in times of crisis. He does not believe God can give him answers to his existential problems.

The denominational church is concerned about perpetuation, whereas the fundamental church has a dynamic outreach because it believes man is lost and going to hell. Usually the denominational minister is more concerned with "keeping the church going," rather than aggressively reaching the neighborhood for Christ. Committees and offices were formed by the institutional church to get a job done, where there was the satisfaction of accomplishment. Members volunteered to serve on committees out of loyalty to the Lord or sense of fulfillment in a job well done. But with the passing of time, people accept a job because they want the status, yet they are not willing to pay the price of service. Finally, people are appointed because "nobody else wanted the job."

Members of a denominational church are usually proud of their membership in their religious society. Their spirituality is judged by church attendance and financial support; little is said about hypocrisy and such things as social drinking and dancing. *Attendance* at previously excluded places is no longer considered a part of one's religious life. There is little difference between the lives of church members and non-church members. Discipline or expulsion of members from the church is never mentioned. Most know that new members join the church by going through certain formalities, rather than giving testimony of an internal change. Denominational churches have certain status positions that are desired by men in the business community. If a man is an elder in the church, he is respected and usually advances in business. Denominational churches are usually more prosperous than sectarian churches and usually have more of a "cathedral image" in the neighborhood, rather than the sectarian "preaching-house image."

Deterioration of the Denomination

The final stage in the sociological cycle is described as *deterioration* which also has been called institutional blight.[22] Inertia settles through the social life of the movement when a denomination has been in existence long enough for the primary responsibility of individuals to slowly shift to professional clergymen. Individuals, committees and officials lose sight of the original goals of the founding fathers. Formalism seeps into the group vitality. The leadership spends more time keeping the organization going, than in making new converts. The control of the denomination slips into boards and committees that tend to become self-perpetuating. Nominating committees perpetuate incompetency by bringing in ballots packed with cronies, rather than competent candidates. If a young pastor asks embarrassing questions, he is ignored in elections. Candidates are chosen on the basis of their loyalty to the denomination.

Leaders at denominational headquarters, removed from the local church, feel they can lead the churches into new programs of action, whether or not instigated or endorsed by individual congregations. After all, the people are sheep to be led; therefore, new programs of action are inaugurated whether or not the people respond. Shaler observed:

> The inevitable decline of congregational economy and the accompanying socialization of the decision-making process within the hierarchy of the denomination is not necessarily a deplorable trend. While it is true that power has a corruptive influence, it is also true that independence has encouraged irresponsibility.[23]

The long evolution towards centralization of church authority makes for both a stronger and weaker sect. Denominationalism does make the outreach stronger, but leads to the inevitable weakening of commitment on the part of the individuals.

Meaning of the Mergers

The ecumenical merging of denominations is unparalleled in church history. Groups have always splintered rather than merged. However, many observers feel that the merging of denominations is an effort to save deteriorating headquarters from oblivion. Leaders feel that consolidation of headquarters, reduction of overhead cost can eventually save the denomination. However, the ecumenical movement minimizes doctrinal distinctives, along with ignoring traditional loyalty to the primary organization. As a result, the ecumenical movement alienates members at the local church level.

Another reason [24] for the breakup of denominations is mobility, which has become the American way of life. The wages of change is death. In the past, there was a great amount of stability, when Americans tended to die and be buried in the same city in which they were born. Churches were community institutions, and only upon great persuasion did a Baptist become a Presbyterian or vice versa. When Americans moved from one community to another, they sought out their family church and put their letter in the kind of church where they had been raised. One Presbyterian confessed, "My mother would die if I left the Presbyterian church." The movement of rural immigrants to the city has grown at the same time when denominations are going down in attendance. Many who leave the farm areas are not seeking out a like-faith church to attend when they move to the city. Some farm people believe the cold, impersonal city church is nothing but a social club, hence they do not give their loyalty or tithe to a new church. As a result, many Americans drift away from church attendance. Others have not had their spiritual needs met in denominational churches; these have joined sectarian churches, which explains their rapid growth. In the sect church, they find a "homey" atmosphere like the rural church back on the farm. Also, the sectarian church gives them social recognition. Mann has noted, "By preserving important rural attitudes and values, the sects soften the impact of the strange suburban world upon their members. Urban evangelical expansion may thus be used as a stage in the urbanization of

the rural people with a strong fundamentalist background." [25]
Many of the large fundamental churches up North are filled with
Southerners who have found an evangelistic zeal similar to the
churches in the Bible-belt.

Mobility Aids Fundamentalists

Cultural shock cannot be discounted as a reason for denominational deterioration. When individuals move from one community to another, certain social processes take place. First, the person
is liberated from his former group associations and their expec-
tations. He is free to move in a broader area, with more liberty.
New friends are not as meaningful as the former relationships.
Cultural shock is the result of more impersonalization, decreased
stability and isolation from the world about him. The denominational Christian does not find a warm acceptance in a new
church with the same name where his former membership is
located. As a result he may drop out of church altogether or join
a warm fundamentalist church. The growing mobility in America
will help the fundamentalists while it will decidedly hurt the
mainline Protestant denominations. Moberg notes, "New sects are
often safety valves providing disoriented people opportunity for
reorientation within a new religious system that meets their
particular social and spiritual needs." [26]
The question is inevitably asked, Where do people go who
leave the decaying denomination. Moberg indicates that people
who withdraw from institutionalized or deteriorating churches
drift into new sects or are drifting without any formal church
connection.[27] The thesis of this volume is that these new super-
aggressive churches are the answer to dying denominations.
The Baptist Bible Fellowship is growing rapidly throughout
the South. Most observers maintain they are using the techniques
once employed by the Southern Baptists. As the Southern Baptist
Convention has become more institutionalized, it has gradually
drifted away from the evangelistic preaching and their Sunday
Schools are no longer evangelistic classes; they have become
"religious romper-rooms" to give children an experience in the
Word of God. The Baptist Bible Fellowship is employing the
soul-winning techniques used by the Southern Baptist Convention

20 to 30 years ago. The rapid growth of the Baptist Bible Fellowship, along with the leveling out of the growth indicated among Southern Baptist churches, shouts a message to the denominational leaders in Nashville.

CONCLUSION

The cycle is inevitable, but at least not for two or three generations. The sociological cycle shows that a fundamentalist/sectarian church is founded upon warm commitment to God and a deep desire to proselyte new members. In order to make the church more effective, it is organized and procedures are streamlined. Professionals are hired to expand and improve the ministry. Churches realize they can do more with an efficient central organization. Little do the members realize that the organization effort both kills and saves.

Churches can go through the cycle sociologically and not theologically. A small fundamentalist church may be committed to biblical evangelism. The congregation gives much time to guarding its doctrinal statement. The pastor maintains, "We must be pure." As a result, the congregation ignores methodology and slowly the life-style of the church changes. Its fervency is eaten like cancer from within, but the doctrinal creed is never touched. The church moves on the cycle.

What can be said for dead orthodoxy? Jerry Falwell states, "To be dead is dead, whether a church is liberal or G.A.R.B. (General Association of Regular Baptists)."

At the same time, a liberal Sunday School mission can give lip-service to humanized theology, yet have some sectarian traits. Therefore, a church must examine its entire life, not just doctrine, to determine if it is carrying out the aims of the New Testament.

Churches tend to reflect more than one stage of the cycle at the same time. Some super-aggressive churches are highly organized, yet functionally evangelistic. Some churches are similar to sects in certain departments, while other departments of the church are institutionalized. According to Moberg, "The five stages in the church's life cycle overlap." [28] The predominant characteristic of a church determines where a church should be located on the cycle.

The cycle seems to be inevitable. No church has remained pure since its inception. Every church has eventually gone liberal —every church. Just as churches inevitably deteriorate, so do Bible colleges, seminaries, mission boards and all other Christian organizations.[29] The cycle is inevitable because of the sinful nature of man, the principle of leaven in society and a natural drift of the world from supernatural to secularism.

The obvious question follows, "What can be done to save our churches?" The first answer is to return to the biblical mandate of a New Testament church . . . return to soul winning as commanded in the Great Commission. The second observation, place emphasis on reaching people, rather than building organizations or constructing buildings. (At times organization and buildings are needed to minister to people, but they are *means,* never the purpose of a church.)

The judges of Israel were constantly plagued with the problem of dying religious devotion.

> And the people served the Lord all the days of Joshua, and all the days of the elders that outlived Joshua, who had seen all the great works of the Lord, that he did for Israel. And Joshua the son of Nun, the servant of the Lord, died being an hundred and ten years old . . . And also that generation were gathered unto their fathers: and there arose another generation after them, which knew not the Lord, nor yet the works he had done for Israel. And the children of Israel did evil in the sight of the Lord, and served Baalim (Judges 2:8–11).

When Israel sinned, God raised up a leader to bring people back to Him. "Nevertheless, the Lord raised them up judges which delivered them" (Judges 2:16).

The answer to the sociological cycle is simple. (A simple answer is never shallow.) As a church moves around the cycle, it should place priority upon explosive growth, yet embrace the efficiency of organization. By a clear understanding of the dynamics within the church, a congregation can maintain its zeal, yet not allow growing institutionalization to be the albatross that plunges it into deterioration.

NOTES

1. Elmer Towns, *America's Fastest Growing Churches,* (Nashville: Impact Books, 1972), p. 153.

2. Ernst Troeltsch, *The Social Teaching of the Christian Churches,* trans. by Olive Wyan (London: George Allen and Unwin, 1931), 2 vols. An outstanding analysis of the factors that cause deterioration in churches.

3. David O. Moberg, *The Church as a Social Institution,* (Englewood Cliffs, N.J.: Prentice-Hall, inc. 1962), p. 122.

4. Troeltsch indicated he received inspiration for his sect-church distinction from Max Weber's 1906 work *Protestant Ethic and the Spirit of Capitalism.* Weber said that the sect member reflected the morals of a movement whereas members of the established denominational churches are members because of their birth. Hans H. Geuth and C. Wough Mills, *From Max Weber: Essays in Sociology* (New York: Oxford University Press, 1946), pp. 287–88, 305–6, 313–19, 450. Also consult J. Milton Yinger, *Religion in the Struggle for Power* (Durham, N.C.: Duke University Press, 1946), p. 19–26, 219–27.

5. Moberg, *op. cit.,* p. 100.

6. I am often asked to evaluate certain churches and place them on the cycle. A church is judged by a number of factors rather than one isolated principle. It is possible for a church to reflect more than one phase of the cycle at a given time. I discuss the cycle at length and apply it it Sunday School in my book *America's Fastest Growing Churches* (Nashville: Impact Books, 1972), Chapter 11. I apply the cycle to youth work in my book *Successful Biblical Youth Work* (Nashville: Impact Books, 1973), Chapter 2.

7. Satan is the god of this world (II Cor. 4:3,4), all nature is under the curse (Gen. 3:17), man is sinful by nature (Rom. 3.23; I John 1:8,10), and no effort can justify man in God's sight. Therefore, the fundamentalist judges that a theological perspective of the world and society is the actual basis to relate to life about him.

8. Moberg, *op. cit.,* p. 82, 83. He summarizes the study by Liston Pope, *Millhands and Preachers* (New Haven: Yale University Press, 1942), p. 118.

9. Liston Pope, *Millhands and Preachers* (New Haven: Yale University Press, 1942), p. 124–40.

10. Elmer T. Clark, *The Small Sects in America,* Rev. Ed. (New York: Abingdon-Cokesbury Press, 1949), pp. 218–31.

11. Elmer Towns, *The Ten Largest Sunday Schools* (Grand Rapids, Michigan: Baker Book House, 1969).

12. Elmer Towns, *America's Fastest Growing Churches* (Nashville: Impact Books, 1972). The eleventh chapter explains the sociological cycle and examines the sectarian nature of ten churches in the book.

13. Carl F. H. Henry, "Dare We Renew the Controversy?", *Christianity Today,* June 24, 1957, pp. 23ff.

14. Carl F. H. Henry, "What Is Fundamentalism?", *United Evangelical Action,* July 16, 1966, p. 303.

15. Arnold Hearn, "Fundamentalist Renaissance," *Christian Century,* April 30, 1958, p. 528.

16. William Hordern, *New Directions in Theology Today,* Vol. I., Introduction, (Philadelphia: The Westminster Press, 1966), p. 75.

17. *Ibid.,* p. 76.

18. Moberg, *op. cit.,* p. 77.

19. Alvin W. Gouldner, "Organizational Analysis," Sociology Today, Robert K. Merton, Leonard Broom, and Leonard S. Cultrell, Jr., Eds. (New York: Basic Books, Inc., 1959), pp. 400–28.

20. Moberg, *op. cit.,* p. 97.

21. *Ibid.,* O. 77, 78.

22. Lyle Schaller, *Planning for Protestantism in Urban America,* (New York: Abingdon Press, 1965). Schaller views institutional blight as the spiritual bankruptcy of inner-city churches, which is expressed by purposeless existence.

23. *Ibid.,* p. 211.

24. The main reason for deterioration in the sociological cycle is bureaucracy. See chapter "The Rise and Fall of Denominations" for other reasons why denominations are dying.

25. Moberg, *op. cit.,* p. 107.

26. *Ibid.,* p. 109.

27. *Ibid.,* p. 122.

28. *Ibid.*

29. I gave this lecture for a class of elderly people at Moody Memorial Church, Chicago Illinois, (founded by Dwight L. Moody), and I indicated their church would one day go liberal. They were polite but informed me I was wrong.

CHAPTER 8

The Super-Aggressive Churches

Some churches resemble the small corner grocery store, built on personal service and convenience to the family. The neighborhood store was never intended to service the entire city; the owner was satisfied to provide a living for the family. Many an owner lived over his shop. He received an inner satisfaction that comes to the craftsman who has done his job well. Each regular customer was called by his first name and each order was given personal care. Those who purchased groceries knew the price might be cheaper down the block, but the proprietor was a personal friend. Customers felt an obligation to buy from him at the friendly corner store.

Some small churches resemble the corner shop. Members attend for various reasons, both to fulfill real needs and satisfy unconscious desires. The members know one another and the pastor calls each by name. Warm friendships develop and become secondary reasons for continued participation. The small corner church preaches the same gospel as the large church, but members "feel" satisfied by sitting in the pew and having their children attend indoctrination meetings. They feel uncomfortable in a downtown church. Their disequilibration is difficult to describe, but this inner feeling becomes the basis for choosing a church.

In a small church, the member gets involved; he serves on committees, mows the lawn and expresses his convictions when the board of Christian education changes curriculum in V.B.S. The church building is the extension of his personality, and criticism of his church is an attack on his character.

131

The next church is similar to a gas station. The motorist pulls in and yells, "Fill 'er up!" He expects the windshield to be washed, the oil to be checked and the gas to be high octane. The motorist doesn't call the pump attendant by name, nor is he concerned about his welfare. When he says. "How are ya?" it's simply passing time until the tank is filled. The customer doesn't care if the grease rack is filthy or the building is painted properly. The service station is convenient; it gets the job done.

Many members treat their churches like service stations. They pull in on Sunday morning to be "gassed up" for another week. This person doesn't want to get involved, nor does he care about the particulars of his church. He superficially greets the minister and nods to those leaving church with him. He heartily sings "Safely Through Another Week," for the words express his sentiments.

Other churches are like insurance agencies. A life insurance policy is necessary; everyone should be covered. When an agent calls in the home or the customer drops into the office, all the forms are filled out. The applicant does exactly as told—he signs on the dotted line and writes out a check. When they separate, the customer and insurance salesman may never see one another again. An annual premium is paid and the insurance policy is safely deposited till death; then the insurance company is contacted to collect the premiums.

Religion as "Insurance"

Many Americans treat their churches like insurance policies. When faced with the alternatives, a person accepts Christ or does whatever the minister asks. He attends church to get his name on the roll and he is present to answer appropriate questions or make required gestures. Thereafter, the member may attend once or twice a year. The minister is called only upon necessity, such as during hospitalization, potential divorce or a death in the family.

Other churches resemble the large shopping center with many stores, massive glass picture windows, acres of parking and packed shelves representing a wide variety of items. The customer who shops K-Mart does not care whether he knows the owner; he simply wants the products at the lowest possible price. The small specialty shop only handles one item. The supermarket is convenient—it saves the busy housewife time; all of her food necessities are located under one roof, saving her from driving all over town to get those things on her shopping list. Volume-buying keeps prices low. Mass advertisement and efficient customer procedures attract multitudes, making possible lower prices. The shopping center is an American invention to meet the needs of a massive, mobile population.

The decade of the seventies has seen the rapid growth of shopping-center-type churches with their multiple services to members. Four years ago the author predicted the growth of this type of church during the seventies. Many who read his prophecy in *Christian Life* Magazine laughed at the prospect. The Eastern Liberal Press Establishment was giving news space to the revolutionary church, the Bible study in the living room or charismatic meetings in the basement of Catholic churches. But the reality of large churches grows each month. Dr. Robert Schuller, of Garden Grove (Calif.) Community Church (attendance, 1,913) reflects:

> If I am alive by the year 2,000 . . . I expect to be addressing a group of young ministers and saying to them, "while it is a thrilling thing to feel the power and the impact of the enormously strong church in America today, some of you would never believe that in the 1960's and the early 1970's leaders in the church were predicting its demise. They were predicting that the church of the future would be away from ground and buildings into small homes and private cells and commune groups. How wrong they were. Only the established churches with buildings and staff and people and program can form a base for operation for generations to come. (*Decision,* March 1971).

The super-aggressive church is God's answer to the unique needs of America. This church is not a traditional part of a denomination and its very function repudiates the services offered by denominational headquarters.

The super-aggressive chuch is more than just a large auditorium with wide paved parking lots. It is not the traditional church, expanded for larger crowds to hear a sermon. The super-aggressive church differs from what is expected on Sunday morning. Its aims are broader; its rationale is grounded in the book of Acts and the authority in its church government is unique.

The super-aggressive church stems from the pages of Scripture. It begins with vision and burden. These churches have their roots in the mystery of the supernatural. Since God always works through men, the church begins with a man who has a *vision* of what God can do in his town; then the *burden* grows that God wants him to reach his community with the gospel. The super-aggressive church is large in the heart of the leader long before it expands on the street corner.

The super-aggressive church does have warm relationships, as suggested in the "corner-grocery church," but its focus is on the outside world. It attempts to organize its activities to reach the entire community with the gospel in any way possible.

The super-aggressive church does want to feed its Christians every Sunday morning, as pictured in the "gas-station church," but it doesn't want members just to drop in; every member is expected to get involved in some way in the work of soul-winning.

The super-aggressive church has more to offer than assurance protection against the fires of hell; it attempts to meet every spiritual need of every Christian. It provides more services to all members through employing a number of specialized authorities and organizing specific programs to carry out this aim.

The super-aggressive church was pictured as a large shopping center. Like the New Testament types, every parallel from the Old Testament cannot be pressed into meaning. So every parallel between a shopping center and a church cannot be pursued. Some clerks in large department stores treat customers briskly, and when a disgruntled shopper tries to correct his monthly statement, he feels dehumanized by a computer that ignores his request. But most clerks have human desires, like their customers, and treat them accordingly. Most of the clerks I talk with smile and try to be helpful. Most managers want to handle disgruntled customers, lest one criticism become a tidal wave. They realize the computer is only a tool to service people.

The super-aggressive church is not just a large congregation.

Super-aggressiveness involves an attitude and philosophy. Many super-aggressive churches are small, but all intend to grow. Dr. W. A. Criswell declares, "There is nothing wrong with a small church—we were all small at one time. But there is something wrong with a church that isn't growing."

The Pomerado Road Baptist Church, Poway, California, is a growing congregation. When Pastor Jim Johnston came in September, 1969, the Sunday School averaged 60 persons and the offering averaged $600 per month. During the Spring, 1973, Sunday School reached 1,000 and monthly offerings averaged $6,000.

"We are a testimony to small churches with meager finances and only a handful of workers," replied the pastor. The infant California church exploded by mobilizing the small work force of dedicated laymen, utilizing army barracks, overhauling abandoned school buses and using every available means to reach every available person at every available time.

"The streets belong to Christians," announced Johnston, who still sports his crew-cut from air force days. "The hippies, blacks and students have marched in the streets and Christians sit at home and watch them on TV."

Johnston organized his 97 lay workers to "walk the blocks," ringing doorbells and reaching people for Christ. The super-zeal of Johnston spills over through his workers. Even though the church has been small, they plan to average 5,000 in Sunday School within five to seven years.

The super-aggressive church is committed to area-wide evangelism. The primary purpose of a local church is to carry out the Great Commission and preach the gospel to every person in the world (Matt. 28:18–20). Making disciples (followers of Christ) is the chief task of a church, but not its only task. The church that is evangelizing the lost also must effectively educate its own, for there is a reciprocity between the two aims, because the church that does not properly educate cannot effectively evangelize. Christ said to preach the gospel to the entire world, but to begin at Jerusalem (Acts 1:8). Jesus voiced these words on the Mount of Olives as He overlooked the Holy City, thus giving priority and strategy to the disciples, which was simply first to evangelize the town in which they were located, before going elsewhere. If each church carries out this command, it will first evangelize the area in which it is located.

In the past, local churches have been unable to evangelize their entire city because of distance. For centuries there was no mass transportation. Fifty years ago the commuter train and streetcar brought some people to church. But such transportation to church was a drop in the bucket, compared to the masses. Before the automobile and the highway system, the gospel had to be taken where the people were. Branch Sunday Schools, mission churches and street meetings were used to evangelize the multitudes.

Distance forced churches to band together in an evangelistic outreach. Thus denominations were born out of necessity to evangelize the masses. New Sunday Schools needed a superintendent to supervise their growth. Infant churches needed Sunday School literature, financial assistance and guidance in their growth. But extensive mobility in United States society has brought the metropolitan area as close as the expressway. Men drive 20 or 30 miles to work; those who live in small towns now drive 30 or 40 miles to the nearest city to buy groceries. A person can drive as far to church as he drives to work.

Why Have Denominations?

The super-aggressive church has eliminated many of the reasons for a denomination. First, the energetic church has a commitment by its leadership to confront every person in the city with the gospel. Second, the growing church has the voluntary manpower to visit every home in the area to reach people. Since the aggressive church is built on an effective organization, it usually has a structured visitation program that follows up prospects and presents the gospel to the lost.

Third, the church attempting to saturate the city has a financial base to purchase time on radio and TV and space in the newspapers. Along with financial base comes an ability to purchase Sunday School buses, educational equipment and to erect new buildings. Landmark Baptist Temple, Cincinnati, has over 100 buses used to reach into that metropolitan area each Sunday morning, some of them going 40 miles in one direction. Finally, the large church has the community acceptance to conduct special evangelistic rallies that attract multitudes. The Thomas Road Baptist Church will attract more to its evangelistic meetings than all of the other churches in its city could gather in a city-wide cooperative program.

Paul planted super-aggressive churches on his missionary tours. We do not find him specializing in the small hamlets or rural areas; even though he visited these areas (such as traveling the island of Cyprus, from city to city, Acts 13:4–12), Paul spent most of his energies in major metropolitan areas of Asia Minor establishing churches. He spent time in Ephesus, grounding the church in the Word of God: "And this continued by the space of two years; so that all they which dwelt in Asia heard the word of the Lord Jesus, both Jews and Greeks" (Acts 19:10). Note the emphasis on "All they which dwelt in Asia heard the word." Jesus had commanded to go to *all*, but how did Paul accomplish this phenomenon? He later testified, "that by the space of three years I ceased not to warn everyone night and day with tears" (Acts 20:32). He reached everyone in Ephesus by organized visitation: "And have taught you publicly and from house to house" (Acts 20:20). His burden (tears) for people and vision of what God could do for them motivated him to visit every home in Ephesus. Many became Christians, and as they traveled throughout Asia Minor they spread the good news. The key to area saturation was an aggressive leader and a strong local church.

A Very Mobile Church

Today's super-aggressive church is not limited to a neighborhood. It can cross into different ethnic neighborhoods, much as a radio signal crosses city limits and reaches an entire area. The Federal Communications Commission does not allow a TV station in every small community, but allows a powerful channel to flood an area with programs. Just so, the aggressive church can reach several communities, crossing ethnic and color barriers. The liberals talk much about integration, but with tongue in cheek allow *de-facto* segregated churches in lily-white suburbs. The only blacks they ever see are colored in the pages of the Sunday School quarterly. The churches with Sunday School bus outreach have gone after children of all colors to bring them to hear the Word of God. They bus them across socio-economic barriers because the gospel destroys such boundaries. When the author observed a number of blacks at the United Baptist Church in San Jose, California, he asked Pastor Larry Chappell how many were attending: "We don't have any blacks; all we have are Baptists," was his reply.

Since mobility is a way of life in America, the magnetic church can pull its members from every suburb in the large metropolitan area. Many of these large churches testify that they have people coming from surrounding towns, such as the First Baptist Church, Dallas, Texas, which claims that people drive from Sherman, Texas, some 50 miles away. The outreach of radio, TV and the newspapers supports the evangelistic outreach of the church, enabling it to spread the gospel in many areas of the city that could not previously be reached by the small church.

The day of the small neighborhood geographical parish church seems to be passing away. In a recent study by the Presbyterians, it indicated 76 percent of those who joined the Presbyterian churches in Pittsburgh, Pennsylvania, passed another Presbyterian church on their way to the church of their choice. Individuals do not choose a church based on nearness but rather the aggressiveness of the pastor, the friendliness of the congregation or the help they get from the sermon.

There was a day when many people chose a new church by previous denominational affiliation. They moved to a new community and began searching for a certain denominational church like the one they attended back home. However, in the past 20 years denominational allegiance has crumbled. People now choose churches for varying reasons. The large first downtown church was chosen for its respectability, while the small corner church was chosen for its friendliness or convenience. Even though most Americans refuse to admit it, Sunday morning *was* the most segregated hour of the week; the rich worshipped together, as did the poor, blacks with blacks, and Orientals sought out their own. However, an aggressive church breaks down socio-economic barriers.

Bigness has become a way of life; all classes and kinds of

people attend a football game, the concert or public schools. The larger the social gathering, the less apparent the social differences. In a large church, social class does not usually elevate one man over another. In a typical board of deacons meeting, one might find a cab driver sitting next to the vice-president of a local bank or an IRS man sitting next to a carpenter. Super-aggressive churches have integrated the races because of extensive Sunday School bus outreach. The congregation has a commitment to reach the entire city, and Sunday School buses cross color and socio-economic lines to bring all children to Sunday School. Black children freely play with those from white suburbia. There is usually no tension felt on Sunday morning, whereas on Monday, children from the same neighborhood may riot in high school because of racial tension. Where public education cannot bring the races together, soul-winning becomes the harmonious catalyst.

The Virus of Bigness

America has been vaccinated with a complex of bigness. We live in an age of sprawling shopping centers, conglomerate corporations, and big business. Most Americans realize that institutions by the masses, for the masses, are for the good of the masses. Jobs and prosperity have been provided for our nation. Public schools have been consolidated to offer quality education to all children, whereas the small school district pressed an unequal yoke upon our children. Since the universities, the military and the government are all big, "What's wrong with the big Sunday School?" asked Jerry Falwell. Falwell indicated that if the church stays in the horse-and-buggy days, it will lose the respect of the public. He states, "Growing businesses have served the needs of individuals and the masses continue to buy at K-Mart. The church can overcome impersonalization and minister to individual need." Even though we don't know the name of clerks at the A & P, we find them friendly and polite. The church ushers can be friendly to all who attend the services, although they can't call them by name. Dallas Billington pastored the world's largest church at Akron Baptist Temple and one Sunday he gave the invitation to come forward and join his church. Billington said, "Some of you folks don't want to join my church because it's too big . . . then you won't like heaven, 'cause it's going to be big up there."

Many feel nervous and uncomfortable in a church service. Anonymity has conditioned the lives of many Americans; people don't want to get involved with their fellowmen. They feel embarrassed to meet a number of strangers. The small, friendly church poses a threat to them, whereas they are willing to attend a larger church where they can hear the proclamation of the gospel without becoming personally involved.

There was a time when the corporate effort of many churches could exert an influence on the political and social life of the community. After the turn of the century, churches got together in a letter-writing campaign, resulting in lobbying efforts on Congress which brought about the prohibition of selling alcohol in the United States. The effort was more than letter-writing; churches worked together in elections, endorsed candidates, resulting in far-reaching legislative impact on our nation. Today, however, when the denominations speak, their voices seem hollow and little heed is given to their message by lawmakers. Perhaps legislators have learned practically that denominations are deteriorating, which is reflected by two facts: First, what the denominational leaders are saying is not the opinion of the man in the pew; or, second, denominational leaders have lost influence on their members. But in contrast, lawmakers will listen to anyone who has power and represents a segment of society. While denominations are losing influence among legislators, politicians realize that some local churches still exercise significant influence over their people. Some politicians who give testimony to Jesus Christ have appeared in large churches and in return have received support from their membership. Senator Thomas Eagleton and Lt. Governor Hearn, both of Missouri, have both appeared at the Kansas City Baptist Temple in special services. Lieutenant-Governor Lester Maddox is an ordained Baptist lay minister and speaks in many churches, as he did when he was the governor of Georgia.

Power of the Church

Two years ago the Junior Chamber of Commerce petitioned the Lynchburg City Council to expand the liquor laws concerning hours and conditions under which liquor is served by the drink. Jerry Falwell mounted a letter-writing attack, and spoke out in his sermons against expanding liquor by the drink. His church members turned out for the city council hearing. They expected the vote to be close, but the pressure was so strong that the vote was nine to nothing against the expansion of the liquor law. A city of 54,000 people cannot ignore the opinion of a church with over 10,000 members.

The large church has its specialists to minister to the many needs of individuals in the many areas of society. Dr. Greg Dixon, pastor of Indianapolis (Indiana) Baptist Temple, has indicated that a sick person from his church will get more and better visits than Christians from any other church in the city. Recently a member commented to Dixon when he made a hospital visit, "Oh, it's so wonderful to have *all* these fine pastors!" Seven different pastors had visited her in her interim in the hospital.

Four years ago students at Trinity Evangelical Divinity School, Deerfield, Illinois, completed a research project that revealed the average church member was on a speaking basis (calling people by their first names) with approximately 60 individuals, whether the church had 60, 600, or 1,000 members. A person's involvement with other members has nothing to do with the size of the church; people can only have an in-depth relationship with a few friends and can carry on an acquaintance with about 60 other persons.

Some view the multi-million-dollar budget of aggressive churches and indicate that the cost is too expensive to run the organization, when in actuality it is more efficient than a small church. With many people sharing the financial burden, each person has to contribute less to the capital expenditures, allowing the church to give more to foreign missions, benevolence, and evangelistic outreach.

The Super-Aggressive Pastor

Not every man is capable of building a large octopus-type church outreach, with diverse ministry into several areas of society. Throughout history, the greatest works for God were done by the greatest men. When the world was given over to sexual sins, God used Noah to save the world. Later, when the world was given over to idolatry. God called one man, Abraham, to form a new nation. Famine struck and the world was starving; Pharaoh didn't choose a council of economic opportunities, he chose Joseph to save the world from starvation. Later, the work of God was advanced through Moses, David and Elijah. In the New Testament, God used the apostle Peter and Paul. Outside biblical times, great revivals and times of church-building came through the influence of Luther, John Wesley, and Spurgeon.

God uses great men to build great churches. The super-aggressive church is built on unlimited vision, unlimited outreach and adequate individuals. Bruce Cummons had a vision of reaching all of Massillon, Ohio, and when he founded the Massillon Baptist Temple sixteen years ago in a small storefront building, he might have been ridiculed, because he had a vision of preaching to everyone in the city and building a huge church. Today the 2,000-plus attendance proves that a man with a great vision can build a great church.

A limitless vision produces an unsatisfied burden which results in a desire to saturate the city. Men who have built great churches use every available means to reach the multitudes: radio, TV, newspaper advertisement, mailing, bumper stickers, signboards, Sunday School contests, and any other means that will attract the multitudes.

But techniques alone will not build a great congregation; back of them must be the driving force of God's man, attempting to reach the city with the gospel. The barest necessity for building a super-aggressive church is a hard-driving man.

Sharing the Ministry

God's man must share his ministry with others. He cannot be jealous of co-workers. Great churches are carried forth on the shoulders of many individuals, rather than just the pastor alone. Some of these super-aggressive churches have full-time staffs numbering over 100, while others number over ten, but in both situations the pastor relies on helpers in the ministry. Each man who assists the pastor is a specialist in his own field: the minister of music, the minister of youth, hospital visitors, the Christian education director, or the business manager, plus a number of other specialists all needed to carry forth the ministry. The concept of multiple services is a practical application of spiritual gifts. "Each man hath his proper gift of God" (I Cor. 7:7). Since God has given different abilities to each person, each man should use his special talent to carry forth the work of the church. One man is gifted to preach (I Cor. 12:28), another to counsel (Rom. 12:8) and another to administer (I Cor. 12:28). The large super-aggressive church allows many gifted men to use their talents and, in the final analysis, each church member will receive a broader ministry of gifts, hence each member will grow more.

A superintendent in the Methodist church indicates 80 percent of his parish ministers would leave their church tomorrow if they had any assurance that another church would not confront them with even more vexing problems. Ministers have traditionally changed churches every three to five years. One phenomenon concerning the super-growing church is that the pastor plans to invest the rest of his life in that church. These men have an intense burden for a community and develop strong ties with the people of the church. Pastor Larry Chappell, United Baptist Church, San Jose, California, introduces guest speakers to his audience, rather than the reverse. To the author he said, "I want you to meet the greatest people in the world. I plan to spend the rest of my life here."

For total-area saturation, a minister must invest more than three to five years. Momentum is gained with time, leading to accelerated church growth. At the writing of this book the pastors of the ten largest Sunday Schools in America had an average of 26 years' tenure.

Lack of Competition

When denominations were being formed, there was no radio, TV or other electronic entertainment media to compete with the local church for the attention of church members. Books and newspapers were the primary source of communication. Personal appearance of entertainers was limited. As a result, most in the community attended a church for secondary purposes: i.e., academic stimulation, entertainment, sociability, or to relieve boredom. The minister had a semi-captive audience on Sunday morning when he stood in the pulpit to explain the Word of God. His manner of presentation, as well as his content, determined the effectiveness of his evangelism.

But with the rise of secularism and the decline of denominational distinctives, the basis for preaching has been drastically altered. Liberal theology has gutted many churches of their theological distinctives, causing ministers to look for other reasons for their existence. During the early days of liberalism, sermons dipped into an insipid devotionalism, aimed at reinforcing Protestant values without a biblical base. Ministers still used words such as *grace, faith,* the *death of Christ.* Bible verses were still quoted. Liberalism, looking for a cause for existence, spawned the self-reassurance of Norman Vincent Peale and positivism of Harry Emerson Fosdick. Dr. Jack Hyles, First Baptist Church, Hammond, Indiana, an avid critic of liberalism, characterized their sermons as "stones given to church members who come looking for bread."

In the last 20 years preaching in mainline denominational churches has gradually shifted to social-oriented issues, including voter registration, racial integration, the rights of minority groups, pollution, political issues, and antiwar issues.

Historically, the minister was considered the scholar of the neighborhood. He had the largest personal library and the best education in the community, outside of the community lawyer or town doctor. The basis of his education was scholarly pursuits and a young man was judged worthy of the ministry when he had mastered the original language, systematic theology and possessed a broad general knowledge. The traditional minister usually wrote out his sermon in longhand, after spending 20 hours of study. He was careful to exegete every passage correctly, knowing that the laymen in the pew had at least a "grandmother knowledge" of the Word of God. What the minister said was important, because denominational distinctives were built on correct understanding of dogma and beliefs.

When the biblical scholarship of the pastor decreased, the social-psychological minister emerged into leadership. The new minister had to understand sociology to comprehend all of the institutions about him. He needed psychology to understand the people to whom he ministered. He needed to be skilled in interpersonal relationships and understand group dynamics. He needed to be an expert in advertising. He had to understand "retail marketing" to present Christ individually and "wholesale marketing" to present Christ through sermon and other mass media. The demands upon him forced him more into the secular role, away from the theological scholar. Various expenditures of substantial capital forced the pastor to be a businessman and comptroller at the same time.

This shift in pulpit preaching reflects a shift in the training of ministers. The young theologian in the seminary is no longer required to master Greek and Hebrew, the original languages of Scripture, but rather the thrust is sociology, group dynamics, philosophical assumptions, and textual criticisms. The aim is no longer to produce scholars but activists. The average layman would be shocked, visiting seminary dormitory rooms, to find *Playboy* magazines, a six-pack of beer on the window sill, a pipe on the desk and a frank confession from the future preacher that he should have all-night dating privileges in his room with members of the opposite sex.

The Activist-Oriented Church

Sunday morning sermons have taken a different hue. Biblical scholarship has lost its appeal or, in the words of a Methodist bishop, "the Bible is irrelevant." Sermons in the mainline denominations for the most part are activist-oriented. The modern-day minister reasons that since the Old Testament prophets spoke against social ills, the twentieth-century preacher should make pronouncements concerning the social evils in the American economy. The new theology attempts to reinterpret the Bible in the light of changing issues. Therefore, he attacks what he sees wrong in society: pollution, the industrial-military complex or segregation. The young theologian cannot be faulted; he believes preaching should meet the needs of people both individually and corporately. But the nagging question remains, "What are the problems of society?" Those who believe the Bible maintain man's rebellion against God is the ultimate problem of all men and that personal regeneration is the beginning of the answer. All other solutions are superficial.

At the other end of the pendulum from the liberal minister is the fundamentalist committed to evangelizing his town for Christ. He must be both biblical scholar and activist—soul-winning activity. Two years ago 23 ministers from the Baptist Bible College, Springfield, Missouri, were listed by *Christian Life* Magazine as pastoring churches within the 100 largest Sunday Schools. Most of these men had founded and built large churches within their lifetime. When one examines the curriculum at Baptist Bible College, he finds devoted teachers instructing students from the English Bible; the whole thrust of the school is aimed at equipping future preachers to build great churches. Biblical scholarship is not the only purpose of the Baptist Bible College. Young ministerial candidates are given practical training in how to build "the largest Sunday School in town." Their graduates have been characterized as packing their car the morning after graduation, going to a predetermined town to knock on every door and win people to Christ, with a view to building the largest Sunday School in the vicinity.

Conclusion

The growth of fundamentalists in the past few years has been extraordinary, and they claim that their success is the result of God's blessing. However, fundamentalists have always preached the Word of God but have seldom had the success of these super-aggressive churches. Fundamentalist churches are not the same as super-aggressive churches, but all super-aggressive churches are fundamentalist in doctrine.

The sociological climate of America allows for the unparalleled success of these churches. Large masses of individuals are fed up with the sleeping church and are demanding answers to their questions about God, if not seeking a relationship with God Himself. These churches offer an authoritative solution to the greatest individual need, the need for redemption from sin.

The growth of mobility has allowed man to venture far from the warm home ties and surroundings that reinforce his identity. Fundamentalist churches are built on traditional American values: the Protestant ethic which was grounded in Scripture. Individuals who are now separated geographically find support to their subconscious needs in these churches.

Anonymity has produced "lostness" of modern individuals, who exist in the growing computer jungle. Man rebels at being an IBM number and is threatened by a spiraling depersonalized world. He finds in these churches a wholeness of person, because the core problem of sin is settled.

In America we are experiencing a burgeoning centralization of authority in Washington, D.C. Individuals who make up middle America have less to say about their own destiny than in the past. The social, educational, political, communication and moral issues are determined at the central seat of power; many Americans want to speak out against existential tyranny, yet don't know how. The fundamentalist offers an historically acceptable method of revolting; the "lost" American joins the super-aggressive church and not only finds a self-identity, but discovers an avenue to vent his opinion.

The churches that are growing have a built-in success-thermostat. Ministers proclaim the Word of God frankly and fearlessly. Sin is denounced for what it is doing in the individual and the community. The Word of God is the authority to attack sin. Sinners are told that their main problem in life is sin and that iniquity will send them to hell. God who lived in the ages past sent His Son to be made of a woman, born of a virgin. Jesus Christ was born without sin and lived a perfect life. He died and has become the only mediator between God and man. God's Son was raised from the dead as a vivid token that all who believe shall live forever.

Super-aggressive churches preach this message on Sunday morning; members witness it to their neighbors during the week. Those who want to go to heaven are asked to "walk the aisle," where they ask Jesus Christ to come into their hearts. Liberal theologians may laugh at what they call "unsophisticated emotionalism," but the guarantee of authenticity for fundamentalist churches is the changed lives of those who walk the aisle. At Thomas Road Baptist Church there are approximately 50 men in the congregation who have spent time in penal institutions, but have since accepted Jesus Christ as Saviour. According to one man's testimony in the church, "These ex-cons are among the most honest in our church, because Christ has changed their life."

America needs life-changing churches like these.

CHAPTER 9

Can Denominations Be Revived?

Is America experiencing the first tremors of a renewal, with the full force of an earthquake to follow? Some see certain "spiritual" evidences of a revival in our nation. They point to the "Jesus freaks" and note that last year the hymn "Amazing Grace" was listed in the top 40 songs. The rock opera *Jesus Christ Superstar* continues to set box office records. The underground church has captured the fancy of the *avante garde*. Rumors of the charismatic meetings in Roman Catholic and dead liberal churches persist.

Before we can proclaim a revival in America, we must determine "What is revival?" The well-known criterion for revival given by William Schaff, the church historian, gives guidance to interpret our times.

> A revival reaches a hitherto-unreached people, who return to pure Bible study and practice, advanced by a new methodology, reflect their zeal through folk music, inspired and embraced by lay leadership.

Secularism is creeping into every area of American life. If America has been a Christian nation she is losing all traits of godliness (see chapter 2). The candle that shines brightest, illuminates the darkest backdrops. If we are experiencing a revival, it will be easier to report the movement of God, because of the perverse background in which God moves.

148

1. *A hitherto-unreached people.*—The sound of stirring in the mulberry trees is not in the traditional church. Super-aggressive churches that minister to the man in the street are experiencing results. The middle-class church has become a status institution. The super-aggressive churches have gone to those without. The poor, the moral outcast and the youth are attracted to these super-active churches.

The traditional church of the sacred rest has no appeal. Jesus commanded: Follow, . . . do, . . . come, . . . go, . . . look, . . . arise, . . . preach, . . . witness. Jesus used active verbs to stir people to action. The traditional church receives children through birth and passes them to the next generation. When this is done, churches "lock in" their clientele, but also "lock out" great segments of unreached people.

A majority of those who join the new breed of churches in America come by salvation. Very few come bringing their church letter. Pastor Jewell Smith, Temple Baptist Church, Orlando, Florida, indicated that most of his growth was through conversion. "People don't want to join our church because of our standards; they tend to float to other churches in town." This Florida church practices discipline and last year voted five people out of membership for drinking, gossip and adultery. Smith founded the church 16 years ago with a handful and now an attendance of 1800 gathers in a beautiful new 2500-seat auditorium each week.

2. *A return to pure Bible study and practice.*—There can be no revival without the Word of God giving life to the movement. The super-aggressive church is faithful to the literal commands of Scripture. They believe that when Jesus said, "Go ye into all the world and preach the gospel to every creature" (Mark 16:15), He meant exactly that. They believe this command applies to their church; therefore preachers have gone on radio, buses are sent into every neighborhood, visitation teams are organized, and their criterion for success is aggressiveness.

Proselyting is no problem to a super-aggressive church. They have no desire to steal members; they want to lead people to Jesus Christ. Dallas Billington said, "We don't steal sheep; we steal goats." They don't view a person as a Presbyterian, Baptist or Methodist. He is lost and needs salvation. Therefore, they go after all men.

Not only is there an obedience to the Scriptures, the Bible must be taught in Sunday School; it is preached from pulpits and members are exhorted to read the Word of God every day. The return to giving out the Bible has resulted in conversions. The Bible produces life, and life-changed Christians make up super-aggressive churches.

The Traditional Church Is Dying

This author believes the traditional American church with its Sunday morning worship service is dying. Americans want a faith that is dynamic and motivating; they don't get it from dead churches.

The super-aggressive church is not an American invention. It grows out of the pages of Scripture and portrays the marks of a New Testament church. Many modern movements such as the underground church, the interdenominational organization, the Jesus freaks, have not conformed themselves to God's pattern of the church; therefore God's full blessing is not upon them. If there were a true revival, people would turn to the New Testament church.

3. *New methodology.*—Every revival has been borne along on the wings of innovations to reach people. Under Nehemiah's leadership the people were revived, built the wall and introduced a new methodology of public Scripture reading (Neh. 8:1–13). Under John Wesley, street preaching brought the Methodist movement to England. The preaching chapels grew out of his evangelistic thrust and a worldwide church grew out of the new "methods," hence the name *Methodists.*

Two new methods being used by super-aggressive churches to win the lost are a contradiction to traditional Christianity. First, the Sunday School bus is an organized outreach into the community to bring children and adults under the teaching of the Word of God. Bus drivers, like modern-day Robert Raikeses, maneuver their yellow buses into the highways and byways to transport people to church. A Louisville newspaper describing their ministry, quipped, "Come to heaven and leave the driving to us."

These churches purchase used buses from public school districts who, first, have been forced by court orders into obtaining large fleets, and retiring the buses after approximately 100,000 miles. As the author drives the streets of a strange city, he can always tell a super-aggressive church when he sees the church parking lot filled with buses.

A second method used in the fast-growing churches is the master-teaching plan for Sunday School classes. The traditional Sunday School class meets in a small room about the size of a walk-in closet. Children sit in a semicircle, with the teacher sitting in the center. She usually lectures from the Bible, interspersing lecture with questions and illustrations.

When a church has aggressively reached large groups of children and brought them to Sunday School, many problems are compounded if they are enrolled in traditional Sunday School classes. A new teacher is needed for every ten new pupils; but with rapid growth, trained leaders are not always available. Small rooms are needed, but they usually can't be built fast enough nor is there money for their construction.

So the master teacher plan is used, which is a modified team-teaching approach. The master teacher is responsible for presenting the lesson to large groups of children, with teacher assistants leading discussion in small groups. The master teacher instructs over 200 pupils at Indianapolis Baptist Temple, while the Bible Baptist Church, Savannah, Georgia, divides classes into approximately 50 to 60 pupils per room.

Other new methodology among super-aggressive churches includes church newspapers mailed to unsaved, goal-setting, TV outreach, and paid newspaper advertisement.

4. *Zeal reflected through folk music.*—Revivals have their hymn writers to set the heart of the multitudes to singing. Martin Luther captured the heart of his followers by music, as did Charles Wesley with his 5,000 hymns. Sankey wrote songs for the D.L. Moody revivals.

If we look to the contemporary church scene, we do not find a new folk music (called religious pop music) that is capturing the hearts of Christians. The religious rock music craze among youth is repudiated by adults, even those who are Bible-based and would want to witness their faith by music of zeal and warmth.

Most churches still sing the great old hymns of the past. These great expressions of faith were carved out of the expressions of that day. They have solid theology; contemporary Americans can identify with their doctrine. However, the great old hymns do not express the emotions of today. We still wait for the hymn writer to emerge who will move us as a church to music.

5. *Inspired and embraced by laymen.* Every revival must reach beyond the leaders to the people. The Wesleys, Asbury, Delemonte and the few members of the Holy Club at Oxford were an insignificant minority compared to the Church of England. But through time, these leaders inspired a group of faithful lay preachers to stand behind the pulpits in the Methodist preaching chapels. These men carried the revival to the coasts of England.

Leadership of Great Men

The super-aggressive church movement in this country is led by great men such as Beauchamp Vick, Jack Hyles, Lee Roberson, John Rawlings, Jerry Falwell and other pastors of great churches. But quickly closing rank are thousands of pastors who want to reach their community for Christ. Not all of these men have theological training; many are laymen whom God has raised up to build a large church.

Jack Dinsbeer enrolled one semester at Baptist Bible Seminary, Fort Worth, Texas, and one semester at a junior college in Jacksonville, Florida. He dropped out of both. He became pastor of University Baptist Church, Jacksonville, Florida, with less than 60 in Sunday School. This past fall he averaged over 1200 in attendance and completed a $1,500,000 budget. For a man with a layman's education he has built the 1750-student University Christian School, kindergarten through grade 12, in addition to the Jacksonville Baptist University.

The author is committed to higher education, but he sees that there is more to building a church than college or seminary training. Super-aggressive churches are built by super-aggressive men and for some reason aggressiveness is not learned in classrooms.

The author has coined the phrase "the hot-poker philosophy" for training of young men at Lynchburg Baptist College. The school was founded to train young men to build super-energetic churches. He realized that heat transferred from the fire to the poker; so he said young men should come into contact with the greatest men of God; here the heat passes. Young men become great men of God by associating with great men of God. The typical American preacher who comes from seminary to the pastorate has little direction for his ministry. He's like a lost ball in high weeds. A young man who has associated with a successful pastor has a clear blueprint of what it takes to succeed.

Can Denominations Be Revived?

Periodically, denominations undergo institutional change (not revival), whereby a few superficial changes are made and a new program out of headquarters calls for "every-member commitment" or for a corporate evangelistic thrust "Project-74." These outward programs do little to affect the basic nature of denominational structure and existence. Extra money may be raised and a few additions may be added to the rolls, but basically the downward sweep on the attendance charts remains undeterred.

The prospect of a denominational structured revival is questionable, but all things are possible with God. True revival for a denomination can only come through individuals who return to the original purposes of their churches and display first-generation fervency and sacrifice. If this revival comes, it will require six steps.

First, the leadership of churches and denominations will have to admit that their group has devolved into a stage of "institutional blight," that is, the denomination has come to a place of carrying out the *form* of Christianity rather than the *function* of the New Testament. A group of people must realize their need before they can properly diagnose their condition and move on to a remedy. But can denominational leaders do this? By such an admission, they would deny their own existence.

The *second* step in revival is returning to proper priorities, a returning to the New Testament. God's Word is the only revelation that reveals the nature and person of God. From this revelation comes a basic awareness of the person of God and how He can be approached for salvation. There is no revival apart from the Word of God.

A *third* step for denominational revival comes when repentance spreads to all members. They should be willing to return to the

theological distinctives that brought the denomination into existence. This involves a program of indoctrination and education.
Denominational-oriented groups influenced by secularism and
liberalism have reduced their beliefs to a minimum. Revival demands a stirring of group pride in the distinctives that made the
denomination great.

Emotional commitment is the *fourth* step in reviving a denomination. There is a dialectical difference between the church
and the world. Intellectual knowledge about the Bible will not
cause a man to choose Christ and reject the world. Commitment
to the church of Jesus Christ must come first individually and
secondly on a corporate level. If a Christian has dedication to the
church, he will receive a stigma from the world. The individual
suddenly finds himself out of step with the world, yet in harmony
with those about him in his religious community. Since the
American life is built on conformity, American Christians will
find it difficult to be different in their beliefs and practices from
those who live in the apartment above them or in the same suburb.

Emphasis on the Individual

Emotional commitment emphasizes "individualization," which
means that private Christianity becomes a matter of choice or
preference of the individual who joins himself with other like-
faith individuals to return to their church's foundation. Such
private Christianity, however "real" to the individual believer,
cannot fulfill the classical task of denominations, to bring in a
Christian world; neither can he hope to confine everyone else to
his own beliefs and practices. Revival can never hope to make
America Christian as in the past. But instead of trying to form
walls and carry out social action on the entire society, the true
Christian will, by private Christianity, become the worthwhile
citizen to all of society. He will hold the views of others in
toleration and respect, at the same time recognizing that his view
of the Word of God and the requirements of God are in keeping
with his own conscience and rationality. He will be super-aggressive in attempting to reach the lost, while holding respect for them
as individuals. The Christian will segregate his Christianity into
a private sphere which becomes "functional," yet livable in a
secular world.

Christianity can never hope to become the approved way of life in America, nor can any one denomination hope to build itself into the one super-church and still be in keeping with the Word of God. When a denomination becomes universal, it lacks "reality," and when it becomes "real" it lacks universality.

The *sixth* step in institutional revival is a return to the first days of the denomination—a return to the days when local churches had the loyalty of their members and were the main religious body in America. If denominations would place focus on individual churches there could be a strengthening of the broken walls.

Can denominations be revived? Probably not. The author does not see an institutional revival in America. In the history of Christianity, God does not revive decayed institutions; He builds new ones. Churches that have died are not brought back to life. Christ threatens the seven churches in chapters 2 and 3 of the book of Revelation, "Repent and do the first works or else I will come unto thee quickly, and will remove thy candlestick out of his place" (Rev. 2:5). God does not rekindle old lights; He begins new ones.

God is beginning a new movement of super-aggressive churches across America. His spirit has departed from most denominational churches. His finger etches "Ichabod" over their doors. This new movement of hyper-aggressive congregations spills over theological lines. They are found among the independent Baptists, Southern Baptists, Bible churches, Churches of God, Assemblies of God, Nazarenes and many other groups.

The super-aggressive church is the church of the future.

Appendix

What Is a Church?

As we see the denominations dying, we also see local churches growing in size and strength, characterizing the future as the day of the local church. The doctrine of the local church is the theological battleground of the 70's. Each past generation has fought its own theological battle. Theological issues are covered by neglect or there was no pressing need to determine what God's Word said on a doctrine. But once an issue becomes the focus of controversy, good men examine it carefully, disagree passionately and finally exhaust every shade of meaning. Thereafter the issue still divides good men, but at least the implications of the doctrine are understood. Today's theological battle concerns the doctrine of the church: What is the *ecclesia?* The theological battle of the past decade concerned itself with the Word of God: What is inspiration and inerrancy? The decade before that the issue concerned itself with eschatology: When is the Lord coming, where and in what form?

The burning issue that separates Christians today is the local church. Inasmuch as we live in a pluralistic society, men project their needs and ideas for the church. Each man from a different background devises a different concept of what the church should be. The pages of the New Testament must be carefully read to determine the makeup of a church.

Of course a church is not the building nor is any gathering of Christians a church, just because they call themselves by that title. The word *ecclesia* in the New Testament meant "gathering," and any church must be a gathering of those who are Christians. The term *ecclesia*, mentioned 114 times in the New Testament, could have been better translated in our Bible as "assembly." Whenever we think of the term *church*, let us always primarily concern ourselves with the people who are assembled in the name of the Lord.

A church is an assembly of baptized believers, in whom Christ dwells, under the discipline of the Word of God, organized for evangelism, education, fellowship and worship; administering the ordinances and reflecting the spiritual gifts.

---

1. *A church is an assembly of baptized believers.*—The first criterion for a New Testament church is an assembly of those who have been scripturally baptized according to the purpose and plan of the New Testament. On the day of Pentecost, those who were saved were immediately baptized and they were added to the church. "Then they that gladly received his word were baptized: and the same day there were added unto them about three thousand souls" (Acts 2:41). Baptism became more than an initiatory rite into a local church; it is a symbol portraying the ultimate meaning of the Lord's death. The church is the body of Christ (Eph. 1:22–23). When He hung on Calvary, sinners were placed into the body of Christ, and when Christ suffered vicariously, the penalty of their sins was propitiated because they were in Jesus Christ. Individuals were identified with Christ in His death, burial and resurrection (Rom. 6:4–6). And, as a result, when Christ died, we died with Him: "I am crucified with Christ: nevertheless I live; yet not I, but Christ liveth in me" (Gal. 2:20). Since we were identified with Christ's body at salvation, the symbolism should be carried out when one enters the church, the body of Christ. He is placed into a pool of water as a symbol of being placed in the grave, identified with Christ in His death, burial and resurrection. All people in a New Testament church should profess to be Christians and have been identified with Christ in His work on Calvary.

There will be some in the church who are not saved, as was the case in New Testament times (Acts 8:13–23). However, all should be accepted into the church upon their profession of faith. The church is an assembly of *believers,* and when the church is made up of unbelievers it is no longer a New Testament church.

2. *The unique presence of Jesus Christ dwells in a church.*— Christ is the light of the world (Rom. 8:12), and the primary purpose of the church is to hold up the light in a dark, perverse world (Phil. 2:15–16). The church is more than an organization; it is an organism and its life is Jesus Christ. He dwells in the midst of His people. "For where two or three are gathered together in my name, there am I in the midst of them" (Matt. 18:20). Christ walked through the seven churches in the book of Revelation and commended them for their good works (Rev. 2:3) and rebuked them for their sin and false doctrine (Rev. 2:1). When Christ rebuked the churches in the book of Revelation He threatened to take away their candlestick (Rev. 2:5), which would have been removing the presence of Jesus Christ from the people. When Christ is removed from a New Testament church, it is similar to the shekinah glory cloud leaving the Old Testament Temple. If a group of people do not have Jesus Christ dwelling in their midst, they are no longer a New Testament church.

3. *A church must be under the discipline of the Word of God.* —One of the first religious exercises of the New Testament church after the day of Pentecost was "And they continued steadfastly in the apostles' doctrine" (Acts 2:42). Doctrinal purity is essential for a New Testament church. There is a unique union between Christ and the Bible, both the Word of God. "In the beginning was the Word, and the Word was with God, and the Word was God" (John 1:1). Christ pointed men to the Word of God, for it was their only way to obtain eternal life (John 6:63).

When an organizational problem came up in the early church, the apostles realized that they could not waste time waiting on tables went they should be giving themselves to the Word of God (Acts 6:4). A local church must place itself under the authority of God by placing itself under the discipline of the Word of God.

When the minister gives a positive proclamation of the Word of God, this is positive discipline, leading to correct life and belief. When the minister rebukes a congregation for their sin, this is negative discipline, just as a parent rebukes a child for going too near the fire. Sometimes a parent rebukes by the rod. The purpose of discipline is the positive growth and negative correction of the child. The purpose of discipline by the Word of God is the positive growth and negative correction of the New Testament church. When an assembly of people removed themselves from under the authority of the Word of God, they ceased being a New Testament church.

3. *A church must be organized for evangelism, education, worship and fellowship.*—The purpose of a church is more than a "back-slapping fellowship" of mutual friends. In the early church they "ceased not to teach and preach Jesus Christ" (Acts 5:42). Since the church believed that everyone was lost, it also believed that everyone must receive an honest hearing of the gospel. The church in Jerusalem carried the gospel to every home so that its persecutors could say, "Ye have filled Jerusalem with your doctrine" (Acts 5:28). The early disciples were carrying out the Great Commission. The first obligation upon a church is evangelism. The second requirement was education; it had to indoctrinate the new Christian into the faith. The last part of the Great Commission reinforced this belief: "Teaching them to observe all things whatsoever I have commanded you" (Matt. 28:20).

Next the New Testament both provides fellowship and becomes a place for mutual interaction. Chapters 1 and 2 of I John set fellowship as a standard for Christian behavior.

Finally, worship is required of all Christians. Jesus demanded, "The true worshipper shall worship the Father in spirit and truth. . . . they that worship him must worship him in spirit and in truth" (John 4:23, 25). The entire book of Psalms gives the Christian the example of worship.

The marks of a New Testament church are evangelism, education, fellowship and worship. When a church neglects these ministries, it abdicates its calling.

4. *A church possesses the ordinances.*—Two ordinances are given to the church, baptism and the Lord's table. These are to be celebrated by the church when it assembles together. Even though the ordinances are given for personal edification and testimony, an individual does not partake of these apart from the church.

Baptism reflects one's testimony of conversion, that a person is identified with Christ in His death, burial and resurrection. This spiritual identification with Christ on the cross is reflected by one's identification with Christ's body on earth, the church.

The Lord's table is a means of edification, fellowship and personal introspection. A believer is to examine himself before partaking. God provided the Lord's table to keep His church pure and separated from the world.

5. *A church reflects the spiritual gifts.*—Not every group of Christians is destined to grow into a church. A group of people must be properly baptized, under the Word of God and organized for God's priorities. God then raises up leadership to bring the church into existence. These leaders must have the "spiritual gifts" (I Cor. 12; Rom. 12; Eph. 4). God gives gifted men to a church, and when the leaders appear, it is an indication God wants the people to organize into a New Testament church. "God hath set some in the church, first apostles, secondarily prophets, thirdly teachers" (I Cor. 12:28). "And he gave some apostles, and some prophets, and some evangelists, and some pastors and teachers" (Eph. 4:11). When an organization ceases to have spiritual leadership, it ceases to function as a New Testament church.